COUNSELING  With CONFIDENCE

William D. Barr, Editor

Logos International
Plainfield, New Jersey

To the One who, for over eight years, has been teaching us His special truths. Jesus himself directed me to transcribe and rewrite the materials He was having us teach others. I dedicate this book to Jesus for He is the One who makes *Counseling With Confidence* possible!

All Scripture references are taken from the *New American Standard Bible,* unless otherwise indicated *The New Testament in Modern English* (Phillips), the Revised Standard Version (RSV), *The Living Bible* (TLB), or the King James Version (KJV).

Acknowledgments

My personal thanks go to many people who helped to put this book together. To the brothers and sisters of the first house meetings where we were asked to teach counseling in these new, revealed-of-God dimensions. To the many people who taped the messages and helped us grow more definitive in our teaching. To the counselees who risked believing in what is a radical departure from normal counseling. To the thousands of new people who confirmed that what Jesus does, He does well!

To Ann Thibedeau who helped type a third draft—and especially to Susanne Potter, Okontoe's secretary and office manager who, for nearly a year, worked to create a copy free of errors—our heartfelt thanks.

To George and Kay Morel who gave my wife and me the opportunity to retreat to their home on beautiful Sanibel Island, Florida, so we could complete the manuscript. God bless all who helped make this day come true.

Preface

If you are faced right now with a humanly impossible situation, "Do not fear or be dismayed . . . for the battle is not yours but God's" (2 Chron. 20:15).

"If I cast out demons by the finger of God, then the kingdom of God has come upon you" (Luke 11:20).

These two verses from the mighty Word of God describe the message of this book. Humanly impossible situations face us daily as we minister in the Spirit through Okontoe Fellowship's Ministry Center in Minnesota. In years past there was much fear, and often we would be dismayed until we awoke one day to the truth, "The battle is not ours, but God's." This turned our lives around, and our ministries began to become exciting and filled with what we have witnessed Jesus doing! We started seeing and being a part of the acts of God as He moves to touch His people in need. We ran into Jesus busy at work setting His people free, in ways we had never believed possible in this last half of the twentieth century!

As we started waiting on His commands and orders for battle daily, all of our previous conceptions of how

God works were blown away! We ran into a God who is vibrantly alive, brilliantly directing the battle, ingenious in the ways He changes people before our eyes. Before we came to that day when the wonder of who Jesus is broke in upon us, we were busy "doing the work of God" and too often finding only the work of our own hands rather dull and incomplete. When we awoke to the truth that God is at work and nothing we can do for Him can compare with what He can do through us, we began to rejoice! As He moved upon us through the gentle Baptism in the Holy Spirit, our whole world changed—our ministries came into clear focus—our anticipation of what Jesus would do through us lifted us to heights of joy we had never ascended before!

Gone were the doubts and skepticism of so many years! In place of them, unrestrained excitement was present as we watched Jesus do all He said He would do! Gone were our questions, our wondering what the Word of God really means, our fears that no one can really interpret what God says in the Bible! In place of them, the awareness that the Holy Spirit can and does easily interpret God's Word to those who will believe! No longer were we faced with the book of mysteries, so confusing to the intellectual as well as to the one who "faithed" it all the way. The Bible suddenly opened up to us the life of God—limitless and grand beyond description and ours to explore freely! To open the Word of God, believing it all and realizing we were welcome to plunge to any depth or soar to any height without the restriction of a faith bound by man's limited acceptance of what the Lord of the universe is doing today—left us breathless in anticipation! What if it is *all* true? What if every promise will be fulfilled? What if every miracle will be demonstrated in our lifetimes? What if Paul correctly reported what Jesus had taught him through the school of the Holy Spirit? What if we find Jesus alive in new ways for our time and transferring all His power to continue and go beyond the work He accomplished on earth two thousand years ago? What if Jesus' statement about "casting out demons by the finger of God" still is true today—then "the Kingdom of God can actually come upon us"!

When the "what ifs" were replaced by belief, all heaven broke loose upon us! Out of a struggling campground on the Gunflint Trail, trying to reach people for Jesus, has emerged God's Okontoe Fellowship Ministries. From two families at its beginning, God has now brought seven families, and many single young adults, into an unlimited ministry! A campground to which thousands come to camp, worship, study, and become Jesus' disciples is fast turning into a base for mission to Canadian Indians, as well as a place of discipleship. That mission—clearly spoken to us by Jesus—is one day to reach from "Nome, Alaska, to Hudson's Bay." A ministry center in St. Cloud, Minnesota, which started in rented homes a few years ago, now includes five homes for five families and many young adults. Thousands now are brought by Jesus to this center of His ministry, coming from five different states and finding what we have found—Jesus alive and able to meet the needs of all who seek His counsel. Jesus not only casts out demons regularly but reaches down to touch His hurting people and set them free from all their pains and terrors! Jesus tells us, *"Remember, my plan is to lead you* out *into mission from this place! Here you shall find the base, within the St. Cloud community, to use in my work of outreach across the world!"* With God directing Okontoe, we have no struggle in believing that we will see ministries continue in five states and more, and surely teams will soon be moving out across the world!

Many people who have met the living Jesus in our centers and in our seminars have asked us to write a book. Many people who have studied "Counseling in the Spirit" with us believe a book is now needed for those who want to see Jesus at work counseling His people! Jesus has directed me to turn the tapes of many seminars into the present book, so He can reveal more of His ways of working in these days before His coming again.

The seminar leaders are also counselors. They are teamed up with many of the people mentioned in this account. They are the people behind the teachings of this book. These men are the Rev. Mr. William D. Barr, the Rev. Mr. William O. Barr, and the Rev. Mr. Denis Audet—all three are United Presbyterian ministers—and Mr. Darrell Hiatt, psychologist. We are daily involved in what we have reported.

Bill Barr, Sr.
Sanibel Island, FL

Contents

PART I

Counseling in the Spirit

Rev. Bill Barr, Sr.

1
Counseling Before Receiving the Baptism in the Spirit

Counseling has been a fascinating subject to many people over the years. Those of us who are Christians experience the need to share what we believe with others. Most pastors are familiar with the responsibility of trying to help people in their struggles to live meaningful lives. Many of us pastors found ourselves totally inadequate in this area for many years. We learned various techniques. We tried to be listeners. Out of half-truths, we developed an idea of what counseling was supposed to be.

We thought, first of all, that the mind of man was the all-important factor to deal with. We were trained in behavioristic psychology, and we really believed this was the answer to our need to help people. We believed that the mind, if it was simply conditioned right, would always make right choices. Through thirty-five years of experience, I discovered this simply is not true. There are forces other than society, people, and things which impinge upon the mind and spirit of man. There are evil forces, *and* there is God, who is the major factor impinging upon man and bringing him to newness of life. If you disregard these forces as you try to get people free in their minds, you have only shown them half of the truth. God is on the offensive, very much so, in His reaching out to people to bring them to himself. He attacks the enemies of man and brings man to himself.

What I discovered, prior to my baptism in the Spirit (and I counseled for nearly thirty years in this manner), was to be a concerned listener. I rejected the psychological approach to people which said, "You must not impinge your beliefs or ideas upon a person. Rather, as a disinterested person, you should make no response—just help the person discover his own way to normal living." We were taught to repeat to the people what they had said (reflective approach) and get them to deal with their own problems. I found that these techniques were not adequate, and many psychologists agreed with me by saying we have to show empathy. We believed we had to show realistic concern for people or they would not open up about their real needs. So I began to show empathy. I was concerned with people and counseled in this way for many years. People said, "Bill, you really do love me, don't you? You really feel what I am saying." I did just that and carried all those concerns for people for many years. I would come home from counseling people all day, walk into my home, kiss my wife, and say, "How glad I am to be married to you and not to the person I was working with all day!" It was so sad to see the tragedies in other people's lives!

So, we were simply concerned listeners. We were trying to let the people get their sins, troubles, and sorrows out into the open, then to help them handle their difficulties sensibly. You see, that was the basic technique of psychology, and it still is widely used today. There is one prominent addition to this approach nowadays, the widespread use of drugs to tranquilize troubled minds. Just let people see their troubles, get them all out, and then they will somehow be able to handle them and cope with them. All the power to handle such situations, we believed, was in the individual's mind. So, all we had to do was to expose the problem and offer a prayer that God would help them deal with their problems sensibly! That was our whole approach, both theory and technique. I am emphasizing this purposely, so you will not become confused when we talk about our present method of counseling.

The process was one of trying to get the mind quiet enough to find order. We thought if we could just get people to see their situation as it is, they would be able to react intelligently to it. Then we could help them understand how to work with their problems, and they could ask God to help them.

That was what we used to teach. I worked in this way for nearly thirty years. The tragedies which came out of this ineffective approach broke my heart again and again.

Let me illustrate. I discovered, the very hard way, that people do not choose the right answers, most of the time. The Bible shows why this is true:

For we know that the Law is spiritual; but I am of flesh, sold into bondage to sin. For that which I am doing, I do not understand; for I am not practicing what I would like to do, but I am doing the very thing I hate. But if I do the very thing I do not wish to do, I agree with the Law, confessing that it is good. So now, no longer am I the one doing it, but sin which indwells me. For I know that nothing good dwells in me, that is, in my flesh; for the wishing is present in me, but the doing of the good is not. For the good that I wish, I do not do; but I practice the very evil that I do not wish. (Rom. 7:14-18)

This is the same discovery we made in counseling. The counselee would be ready to accept the situation as it was and would agree to move in the direction of freedom—but he would not have the power to do so! There was the will but not the power.

Does that ring any bells? It rang cathedral bells in me!

But if I am doing the very thing I do not wish, I am no longer the one doing it, but sin which dwells in me. I find then the principle that evil is present in me, the one who wishes to do good. For I joyfully concur with the law of God in the inner man, but I see a different law in the members of my body, waging war against the law of my mind, and making me a prisoner of the law of sin which is in my members. Wretched man that I am! Who will set me free from the body of this death? (Rom. 7:20-24)

This passage is a diagnosis from the Word of God of the very thing we discovered after trying to work in the area of the mind only, trying to get people to choose to live. They had the will to choose, but not the power to change. That makes a world of difference. We had people—always in conflict—struggling all the time within themselves.

Through the years we dealt with many people. I served one church for nine years during two different periods. I had known that church since I was a baby, for it was the church I grew up in. I knew everybody in the church, and many of them had known me since I was in diapers. Many of the elderly women still called me "Billy." It was a unique situation to be able to observe a church over a period of so many years. I saw tragedy after tragedy, even after people had done the things we had told them to do. They went to church. They prayed. They read their Bibles. They went to Sunday school (some were even Sunday school teachers). Yet, when their kids grew up, they would leave home. The parents would come to me saying, "What happened to my kids?" The kids would take off, get into sin and experience tragedies.

We would watch all these things take place and ask "Why?" Why had our advice not been enough? It would break my heart to see such unhappiness. These were kids whom I had worked with. They had heard the truth of God. They had come through the Bible schools and youth groups. Yet, they would choose to do the things which were offensive to God. I would say, "Why can't I seem to get through to you? Can't you see the truth with your minds? Be sensible about it! What's wrong with you kids? Don't you know you're going to get hurt? The wages of sin is death. You're going to die. You're going to have trouble." And they would answer, "But we're going to get away with it!" The mind is devious. It will find a way out. The mind will say, "Oh, it won't happen to me!" All of us have experienced this.

Somehow we had to approach this essential question in a new way. *That* is what God has been teaching us. The Bible says, "If we refuse to admit that we are sinners, then we live in a world of illusion and truth becomes a stranger to us" (1 John 1:8, Phillips). Now that's a very powerful statement! It goes on to say, "For if we take up the attitude 'we have not sinned,' we flatly deny God's diagnosis of our condition and cut ourselves off from what he has to say to us!" (1 John 1:10, Phillips).

You see, in our counseling before the baptism in the Spirit, we were influenced especially by our psychological training. Two major implications of our training were: We didn't believe people were sinning, and, therefore, if we simply could get them into a nice atmosphere, they would make the right choices and would not continue to be in trouble. They would *want* to do the right thing, for their minds would say, "Hey, that will be good. I won't get pain from it!" You see, we had accepted the idea that there really was not any such thing as sin—rather, it was all sickness. Alcoholism, for example, was in this category.

We talked about all kinds of sicknesses which really were sins. These included mental illness (our inability to cope with life), adulterous relationships, and sexual deviations. These were, after all, just sicknesses—or so we thought. We simply must learn to accept them and try to find ways of dealing with them. Our belief brought us to the conclusion that no one really was a sinner—people were just victims of various forms of sickness.

What were the results of this philosophy? "If we do *not* admit that we are sinners, we live in a world of *illusion.*" That is how the Bible says it, "you will live in a world of illusion, and truth will become a stranger to you." And so it was. People were living in their illusions, and I was living in an illusion as I tried to counsel. The encouragement we offered them, telling them they were only sick and would get over it, was an illusion. In effect, we could tell them, "Come on, you're just sick, and we'll help you through this thing." But it was all an illusion, for they were not only sick; they were sinning against God and themselves! There was only one answer to their sin—an approach that was radically different from what we were doing.

2
Counseling After Receiving the Baptism in the Spirit

There are really two important implications to consider when we talk about an individual with a problem being just sick and unable to cope with anything instead of dealing with their problem as sin when sin is involved. First, we are declaring indirectly that we do not need a Savior—a Savior from sin! This prevents Jesus from touching His people in need, for He becomes a stranger to them. If we are not sinners—just people in trouble needing a little understanding, some guidance here, a better living situation there—then, of course, Jesus isn't needed at all. In essence, such a philosophy denies any need of a Savior! If we take the Savior out of life, then we only stay mired in our sins.

The second implication of this approach is that it cuts man off from all the Savior wants to say to him. We cut ourselves off from God's messages to us and cut ourselves off from being saved. The clear-cut answer to many of our problems is found in the Bible: "If we freely admit that we have sinned, we find God utterly reliable and straightforward—he forgives our sins and makes us thoroughly clean from all that is evil"(1 John 1:9, Phillips). Now that is the Word of God, and it is in great contrast to the way we counseled in the past. We did not want to say to people, "You are sinners." The word "sinner," somehow, sounds like an ugly name. It seems so judgmental to say to someone, "You are a sinner." Nonetheless, it is a fact that we are in need of a Savior, and if we refused to admit this, we are in serious trouble—we begin to live in an illusion again.

This matter is at the very heart of Christian counseling. To recognize its truth will open the door for Jesus to touch His people. Without such recognition, you will end up simply being a professional. We have walked away from being professionals in the field of counseling; rather, we try to let Jesus counsel our clients. It would be accurate to say we have become evangelists—taking people to Jesus. As we believe in the power of the Holy Spirit to do the necessary work, we see people's lives completely changed.

I had many counseling failures. Through the years, one thing was very difficult for me to understand. My dear friends would listen to me tell them how happy we were to let God guide us and how well things were going for us. We would say, "Try it, you'll like it"; and they would say, "Bill, if we just had your faith, we could make it!" But this was an illusion, too, because I did not have any more faith than anyone else—just faith for one day at a time. They would look at me and try to follow my ideas, and they would get hurt, because I am not a *Savior*.

When you understand this, you will find yourself in the position of being able to see Jesus help His people, and you won't fall into the trap of saying, "Well, I can tell you what to do about this, you know. That's easy."

Now we sit down with people and say, "Lord Jesus, please speak to these people. Here they are, touch them. Do what you want to do with them. We don't know anything about them." Then Jesus begins to function as the wonderful Counselor.

Previously, we had failed to understand what God had stated long ago in His Word: "A natural man does not accept the things of the Spirit of God; for they are foolishness to him, and he cannot understand them, because they are spiritually appraised" (1 Cor. 2:14). This verse really speaks to the method of counseling we proclaim; it reveals the core dimension of effective counseling.

Now look at the dilemma we face. What man needs is a Savior, but he cannot receive what the Savior has to say to him, if he is going to receive it only as a natural man. If he attempts to do so, it will appear foolish to him.

Let me illustrate this for you. When you tell a man that Jesus can speak to him in clear words, he will frequently answer, "You must be kidding. That stopped way back in New Testament times. No, God doesn't speak today." Such ideas are foolish to the natural man. He may joke and say, "How does He speak to me? Tell me about it if you can." When we explain how Jesus speaks daily to us, he often replies, "I don't believe it." We say, "Well, you don't have to believe it, but until you believe it, you won't hear Him."

This verse is crucial to your effectiveness as a counselor. What we were doing, as we learned more about who Jesus is and how He functions, was speaking spiritual truths to people. The natural man was saying, "You have to be kidding. I can't handle that. What's wrong with you? Tell me something practical to do. Tell me how I'm supposed to love my wife. Give it to me in black and white. Don't give me this business about waiting upon God."

It was interesting. There are two truths in 1 Cor. 2:14 that touched me again and again. The first is that the natural person is incapable of receiving the things of God. This shows us that we should not get mad at people when they can't grasp spiritual concepts. I used to say something like, "Why can't you see it? It is as clear as day. Just open your eyes and look at it." But they could not. They had no concept of what was going on. In the eyes of the natural mind, the things of God are foolish, until he finds the Savior, who turns all of it around and makes it believable.

Secondly, the natural man *cannot* understand the things of the Spirit. You should underline that word "cannot." It will help you to have compassion for the people you are dealing with. It isn't that the person doesn't *want* to understand spiritual truth. The counselee may be like Paul who wrote, "On the one hand, I myself with my mind am serving the law of God, but on on the other, with my flesh the law of sin" (Rom. 7:25). That's the dilemma, and we need to tie this passage from Romans 7 to 1 Cor. 2:14 so we will understand our human condition more fully.

We began to see the truth of the Scriptures more and more. We were dealing with people who were trying to understand in the natural what we were saying. But, we were actually speaking spiritually to them, giving them the truth God had revealed to us. They would simply respond, "Well, I guess I'm too dumb. I just can't understand it." But, when God showed us this verse and underlined the word "cannot," it suddenly put compassion in our hearts, and we said, "Forgive us, loved ones. Forgive us, for we have been trying to teach you spiritual truths which you cannot possibly understand as a natural person, for these are spiritually understood."

There we are again. With our minds we cannot accept the things of the Spirit of God. These "things" are vital to life. They include the following:

1. We are sinners, not simply confused in our minds. That's a spiritual truth—a "thing" of the Spirit.
2. We need to be saved from the evil that is destroying us.
3. Man is created in God's image. He is created spirit, soul, and body; not just body with a mind trying to control the body. You may have thought the soul is the same as the spirit. I thought they were the same for many years, but there is a specific difference shown in God's Word. Spiritually, when you begin to understand the difference, everything opens up.

Everything begins to open, and we begin to see the "things of the Spirit" with our own spiritual eyes. This opening up to the things of the Spirit begins when we discover our need of a Savior—the Lord Jesus! Until we see our need of Jesus, we have only two-dimensional personalities. When our spirits are born again through belief in Jesus as our Savior and Lord, we become three-dimensional people—body, soul, and spirit.

3
Two-dimensional versus
Three-dimensional Man

If we are two-dimensional people, with only bodies and souls, then we are not spiritually able to understand or receive the truth of God. This is what happened when Adam and Eve decided to choose to disobey God and be like God himself. God said, "You shall not eat from it [the tree in the middle of the garden] or touch it, lest you die" (Gen. 3:3). Satan told them, "You surely shall not die! For God knows that in the day you eat from it your eyes will be opened, and you will be like God, knowing good and evil. When the woman saw the tree was good for food, and that it was a delight to the eyes, and that the tree was desirable to make one wise, she took from its fruit and ate; and she gave also to her husband with her, and he ate" (Gen. 3:4-6).

What happened? God spoke the truth. Satan spoke a lie. Adam and Eve chose to believe Satan. They died, spiritually at first; then physical death entered their world. Until then, death had been a total stranger to man. What died? Man's spirit died within him. He was made a spirit (which is man's real being), given a soul, and put in a body. That was God's creation. God intended for man to live forever. That was God's plan. We have no idea how long Adam and Eve lived before the Fall, but they certainly did not disobey God the first day. They could have lived a thousand years in God's joy and peace—total health, no death, fully in the Spirit (understanding "things of the Spirit" with ease). They could have lived on, for man's potentiality as a human being controlled by the Spirit is unlimited. It's a strange phenomenon. There Adam and Eve were—struggling under new terms of life that had been introduced by Satan—and they died spiritually. Then they began to die physically. Cain went out, killed his brother, and saw death for the first time. The world began to go along, limping out of the beautiful paradise of God—limited because people had chosen to become only two-dimensional.

Over the centuries, it has been proved that when a man lives on a two-dimensional level, everything he relates to is on the basis of *emotional reactions*. So, when someone hits us on one cheek and we hear Jesus say, "turn the other cheek," we say, "you've got to be kidding! I'll knock his block off!" Emotionally (body and soul only) you feel such, and physically, you react with violence. This is the natural man in action. But man was destined by God to be a spiritual being, constantly in contact with God. This enables the soul of man to be kept in its proper perspective. When governed by the Spirit, man is still able to relate emotionally—he is able to love and physically capable of expressing that love with his body. He is able to understand that love and able to use his physical body for the joy of God and the happiness of his own family. This was all part of God's plan.

The Old Testament clearly records the lives of many

people who were only two-dimensional. Those who were remarkable leaders, whose lives we look upon with awe, became three-dimensional men by a special move of the Holy Spirit upon them. David, Saul, Samson, Samuel, and the Prophets were amazingly striking people when the Spirit fell upon them. They were three-dimensional people who were able to "accept the things of the Spirit of God"! They did the work God had called them to do, and they changed nations. They shook the very foundations of people's lives. That was God in man. But when the particular work of the Spirit was completed, He did not remain in them at all times (it was like suddenly being "unplugged" after being plugged into God). David did wonderfully well as long as he was God's man—until he got "unplugged." Then he reverted to being a "natural man," devising evil, killing Uriah, Bathsheba's husband, so he could cover his own adultery. David was a king who could have taken any number of wives without shame. But, because he had been a man of God who knew right from wrong, he chose to be devious about it. He acted on his emotional, physical drives, as he became "unplugged" from God and went through the terrible tragedy of having his baby die and Bathsheba caught up in this strange deviousness of the king. Bathsheba was, after all, a woman who could have been taken as wife by the king, for he was king of all. But not David. He was a king under God! This is why David's "unplugged" life was so devastatingly sad.

Every time Samson was "plugged into" God's Spirit he did the most remarkable things, putting the Philistines to shame! But when he became "unplugged," he did the most stupid things imaginable. We must stand in awe of all this, for we see what Samson did vitally when God was upon him, and then when he didn't have God upon him, how he proved himself a total fool!

Well, that's us! What we are seeing is that God had a plan all along to take care of this common human dilemma. It was not until Jesus was sent as the Savior of two-dimensional men and women that things began to come into focus concerning this plan! It came into focus when the Holy Spirit was imparted (a gift of Jesus to mankind) to man and the spirit of man was resurrected! Man came alive spiritually! Born again! Able to begin to receive the things of the Spirit of God! This is the miracle of presenting Jesus to people!

It is dynamic because it is not only the most unusual miracle of all, but it is like having God say, "The plug kept coming unplugged, now let us put a generator inside of man!" This is really the way it is! When the Holy Spirit is within you (like a generator) and your life is submitted to the Spirit, you keep "charged" with God all the time, and your spirit stays alive and able to receive things of God! Then the fun begins!

Now, why have we spent so much time on the two-dimensional-man concept as it relates to counseling? Try counseling anybody without first taking them to Jesus in this new dimension, and you are just wasting your time and their time. You will be building up false hopes in them, too! The persons you counsel must have new spirits within them, in order to be able to receive the truth of God that will set their lives in order!

4

Jesus Counseling His People

Many people say to us, "Why, you can't counsel non-Christians." We reply, "That's true. The non-Christians need Jesus just as much as we need Him, so we, as evangelists, present Jesus to them." This is the basic core of counseling in the Spirit.

To dramatize this urgent need for people who come to us for counseling (some of them come from hundreds of miles away), we sometimes surprise them with a conversation like this. Upon arriving the people will say, "We heard about your counseling center and were encouraged to come here. We are counting on you to be able to take care of our problem."

We will reply, "I am afraid you have the wrong address. We are not the counselors. We will be glad to introduce you to the wonderful Counselor who *will* take care of your problems. But, we are not the counselors. We are simply channels. We will take you to Him. If you are willing to meet the Counselor who will change your life, then come in. If not, please don't waste your time or ours. For there is no other complete answer. We don't have any man-made answers, for Jesus has them all."

A lady came to us who was torn to pieces. She had been through all kinds of counseling—psychiatry, pastoral counseling, friends' advice. All of her "helpers" had agreed that she should get a divorce and "get out of" her bad marital situation. Her lawyer had made exorbitant charges and brought only further confusion and despair to her life. She could not get anyone to give her answers to her plight. After all her efforts, she was a shambles, both physically and emotionally. Someone said to her, "Why don't you go up to Okontoe?" She arrived in a state of near collapse. My son Bill and I sat with her for about two hours, while she told us about her situation, and we simply began weeping. Clearly, this woman had been mistreated and abused. It broke our hearts to hear her story. I finally said, "Loved one, you don't need any more advice. You have had all the advice you need from men. We're not going to give you any more! We have nothing at all to say to you which you can receive just now. Let's go to Jesus." The despair of her situation came crowding in upon us. You simply can't tell people to try this or that when they have been so deeply hurt.

We just prayed, "Jesus, here is one of your own. Touch her in her great need. Help her!"

The next day Jesus began to help her. He took her through a beautiful experience. She received what we call the "Jesus overhaul." It was a beautiful experience to see her come alive—to find real hope. That evening we said, "Jesus, you have done a beautiful job with her, and she is free now from so many things. Just, please, reveal yourself in all your glory to her." We did not know what He would do, but He surely did a remarkable thing with her.

She went for a walk on our nature trail around Arrow Lake. Suddenly, Jesus met her on the path. She

saw Him standing there in front of her, where He
confirmed all He had been doing in her life as she had
been talking and praying with us. He assured her that
she was learning to understand the "things of the
Spirit." She went around the lake to the end where
Arrow Lake joins Shoko Lake. The paths there are
confusing, and she did not know which path to take.
She realized she was getting lost and cried out, "Help
me—help me! I'm lost!" She was all alone out there,
except for Jesus, who was right behind her. He said to
her, *"That's your trouble. You keep going on the wrong
paths. Many of them are dead-end paths, and you
always get hurt."*

She shouted at Him, "Well, what am I supposed to
do?"

Jesus said, *"Turn around."* There was a double
meaning in His words. Physically, she turned around
and found she was on exactly the right path which led
back to Okontoe. Jesus had gone, but she had clearly
heard His voice. Spiritually, she had to turn around
also. She came back, went into the tent camper where
she was staying, and thought, "What in the world is
happening to me?" Then Jesus appeared to her again,
sat down with her, took her in His arms, held her, and
comforted her.

The key in all this is *Jesus.* If you try to counsel any
other way, you will find yourself in deep water. I will
guarantee it. You will be over your head so fast it isn't
funny. The Bible tells us about two-dimensional men,
"Things which eye has not seen and ear has not heard,
and which have not entered the heart of man, all that

God has prepared for those who love Him"(1 Cor. 2:9). This describes two-dimensional men, who are dependent only on what they can see with their eyes, hear with their ears, think with their minds. We could add all the other physical senses into which we have been locked. Such a man is limited! So are we if we remain in the two-dimensional realm.

The following verses explain God's plan: "For to us God revealed them [those "things which eye has not seen and ear has not heard, and which have not entered the heart of man, all that God has prepared for those who love Him"], through the Spirit"(1 Cor. 2:10). Can you see this now? This is the key to becoming three-dimensional people. You become a three-dimensional person when you let Jesus be your Savior and you let His Holy Spirit, who comes to you as soon as you receive Jesus, indwell you. When you begin to let the Holy Spirit take charge of your life, you become a three-dimensional person. Your spirit has been "born." When you are three-dimensional (spirit, soul, and body), you are suddenly able to understand God. This is the whole purpose of counseling in the Spirit. There are no neat and keen little tricks you can teach people, telling them if they do this or that, they will get along fine. I tried that for years. Even when I quoted good things like, "Let not the sun go down upon your wrath" (Eph. 4:26, KJV), it would seldom help. We taught people to settle their differences before going to bed! Good principles—but they would not do it unless they were motivated by the Spirit of God (able to receive the things of God). When God says to them, *"Do this,"* they won't respond to Him, for they will rationalize the need to do so away. They won't know the voice of God, because they cannot understand the things of God until they are spiritually alive.

So, the first work of all counseling is to bring people to a knowledge of Jesus Christ. Let them be spiritually filled, then they can understand what God is saying to them. They won't necessarily be learning truths you may be teaching them. You don't have to list all the Bible verses and suggestions that come to you. God himself will take care of these, if you let the Holy Spirit counsel. Instead, you will be a spectator at a most remarkable experience, as you see God begin to deal with His people. And, in the process, you will hear the Spirit say, *"Turn to this verse."* And you may not have remembered that verse at all. Or the Spirit may say, *"Tell this truth to him"* or *"Ask him this question."* As you do these things, you may see the counselee amazed because the question or verse or truth has impinged, by the power of the Holy Spirit, upon his total life. People, with shocked looks on their faces, will ask, "How did you know about that time in my life?" One woman declared that we must be clairvoyant when we asked her what had happened when she was six years old— the question the Holy Spirit had told us to ask her. We told her we were not clairvoyant but had just this moment responded to God when He told us to ask that question. She replied, "What do you mean, God just told you?" Because of this, we were able to open up for her the truths of how Jesus loves her and knows everything about her—that He was now reaching out through us to touch her and set her free.

5

Four Understandings Necessary to Counseling in the Spirit

There are four basic conclusions that need to be understood before we even consider being channels of Jesus' counsel to His people. First of all, we must proclaim Jesus and His truth, explaining our inability to help people unless the counselee believes Jesus is his Lord. He must turn from his two-dimensional life. Stated simply, we must first proclaim Jesus and let people receive Him. We must lead them along to understanding. We find that people are usually very willing to receive Jesus at the depth of their struggles and great need.

A man came to us whom I loved the first minute I met him. His world was in tragedy. He was really mixed up. Great unhappiness filled his countenance. One of our friends in the Twin Cities sent him to us after beginning the process of opening up Jesus to him. He was an intellectual, and it required hours to get through the mind to the point where he could receive anything spiritual. Most of the first day was spent in going over each step in the process of belief. He would agree after each explanation of God's plan for his life—and he would keep asking for more. I went back to his Catholic background and showed him what his church

27

teaches about Jesus, the Holy Spirit, sin and its cost. He would say, "Yes, I still believe that." I was laying the groundwork for him to be able to believe who Jesus is today. We had good communication going. He could live with what he was hearing. Finally, I reached a point where I said, "The next time before we meet, I want you to go out in a canoe or sit in your campsite and face up to whether you are able to cope with the things of your life that are ahead of you. Ask yourself, 'Am I able to face it alone?' "

I went to his campsite the next day after completing a morning seminar teaching. He was out in his canoe and called to me, "I'm coming!" He paddled in, sat down, and said, "I can't cope with anything."

I said, "Hallelujah!"

He replied, "You're a crazy guy!"

"Yes, now Jesus can come in. You had to reach a point where you could say, 'I can't do it—I need help.' " I told him I didn't have any help for his extremely complex situation, but I assured him that Jesus did. Then I told him to give his life to Jesus right then.

"Well, how do I do that?"

I told him, "Just follow me—I'll take you to Him." At that moment I took him through the prayer of confession into asking Jesus to be his Lord and Savior. He repented of his sins, asked for God's forgiveness, and immediately received it.

Then I said, "Now, let the Holy Spirit quicken you as to what Jesus would free you from. Tonight we'll get together and see how Jesus touches you, heals you, and lays out His answers for your life." That night Jesus did those very things. How quickly that intellectual had reached the point of no return, of realizing there was no help within himself. And Jesus stepped in to bless him, giving him new direction for his life.

That man went home happy, determined to see his life change by the power of Jesus, and no longer alone. The serious matters still before him needed to be faced, and he left us aware that Jesus was alive—not a bit confused by his messed up life and family—and fully able to lead him into a good, new life according to God's plan. He did not have to face these problems alone any more. He did not have to work out the solutions with only his mind any more, since the Spirit of God was now within him. The Holy Spirit would work out the problems still to be faced. We do not send people away with the idea that all is done, but rather we say "Now, let Jesus work in your life."

But some will say, "What do I do if my wife doesn't accept me in my new life?"

We reply, "Ask Jesus."

"Well, what will I do if my runaway daughter refuses to give up her boyfriend she's living with?"

Again we say, "Ask Jesus." You see, our job is to get people to transfer their dependence to Jesus instead of their minds or men's advice.

The second conclusion is to recognize that we are not the counselors—Jesus is. It is important for people to understand we are not wise people with special advice, but rather, we are proclaimers and introducers of people to Jesus.

The third conclusion is that no special techniques do

the job—trying to be empathetic, understanding, clever in trapping people into thinking more clearly, etc. We try all these to no avail—if we ignore the foundation of belief. The recognition that we need a Savior, who is Jesus—the wonderful Counselor—is essential.

The fourth conclusion we have discovered is the need to affirm fully God's truth in Matt. 18:20: "For where two or three have gathered together in My name, there I am in their midst." We have developed a basic principle which we try to follow at all times. We always try to counsel in teams of at least two people. Sometimes, we find ourselves trapped and unable to carry out this plan, but God honors that, too. We counsel in teams because of Matt. 18:20. If we have two at least, Jesus will honor His Word and be in our midst—doing the counseling. We gather in His name, and we declare that right in the beginning of the session.

Let me explain why this is important. When you get into counseling with people a little more, you will need to wage spiritual warfare as a believer in Jesus. You will realize you are not only there to watch things happen, but you are called to be a warrior for Christ in the battle for these people's lives against the powers of evil. As you pray in the Spirit and wait upon Jesus, it is always surprising and exciting to see what He will do. When I use the expression, "pray in the Spirit," I *do* mean using your prayer language silently as you connect yourself to God's wisdom through this vital gift of the Spirit. In practice, we find that as one counselor directs questions to or handles questions from the counselee, the other team member remains in an attitude of awareness while quietly praying in the Spirit. As we do this daily, we have discovered something glorious begins to happen to us as well as to the person being counseled. We become very much aware of God, and our spirits begin to be quickened. Then God begins to use us as channels of His love and healing for His people. God starts releasing His gifts of the Spirit to us in abundance, and we find ourselves using words of knowledge, words of wisdom, discernment of spirits, and often words of prophecy, as God begins to reach out to touch His people. He shows us what is happening in people's lives through these gifts, and we come away more than ever aware that Jesus is the Counselor.

We further believe that when we engage in spiritual warfare against principalities and powers of darkness controlling the people we serve, two warriors are essential. While one takes the offensive against the spiritual enemies controlling the minds of the counselees, the other stands like the Roman soldiers of old—back to back, to keep the enemy from striking from the rear. This is a very real experience of battle, and we remain convinced that Jesus grants His authority to overcome *all* the powers of the evil one, if we let Him move in our midst in power.

Luke 10:1 says, "The Lord. . . sent them two and two ahead of Him to every city and place where He Himself was going to come." This again is the real heart of counseling in the Spirit. If Jesus does not come into the counseling, you had better not go there either!

It is Jesus himself who comes when we go two and

two ahead of Him, expecting Him to come and counsel His hurting people. He does come. It is He, Jesus, who is utterly reliable and straightforward. *He* is the one who forgives our sins. *He* is the one who makes us thoroughly clean from all that is evil (1 John 1:9).

6
Dealing With People's Unbelief

It is so difficult—so agonizingly difficult—when we minister to people who say, "I don't think I really want to try." It is difficult for us when we have people who know the truth of God, then say, "Yes, I know that is the way to do it, but I don't want to do it that way." It's so difficult when people say, "Well, I know God is in this miracle business, but I don't think He's in this business to make a miracle big enough to get me out of the situation I'm in."

This comes to us daily in our counseling. We spend so much time trying to convince people that God is faithful—that He wants to touch them. He has at His fingertips everything they will ever need or desire. But people have been in so many different situations and heard so many different teachings. Some people are skeptical about God's people. As missionaries in India, we heard the Indians say, "Oh, your Lord is beautiful— no question about that. There is nothing wrong with Jesus, but we can't stand your Christians." I'll never forget it. It was a devastating experience to deal with that feeling. They had no fault with Jesus, for He is faultless. He's real! He's alive! For people to finally grasp this fact and let it happen in their lives is one of the things we struggle with. In fact, I think we find ourselves *proclaiming* more than *counseling*—proclaiming the good news of Jesus, and trying to get people to say, "OK I believe you."

We say, "Do you believe it enough to let Jesus do it right now?"

If they reply, "Well, we'll try it," then Jesus touches them and we see miracles happen.

Isn't this what it is all about? It is so important for you to grasp the meaning of this. This is the first thing, to *try to convince people that Jesus is speaking the truth. This will make them stop listening to Old Slewfoot (Satan).* And Old Slewfoot, dumb-dumb—whatever you want to call him—is lying to people today. He's lying loudly! He does it with impunity. He has no restrictions on the way he lies to the people of God either. We can spot him as we listen to people. We say, "You've been listening to Old Slewfoot again, haven't you?"

Now this is in no way a judgment upon the people of God, and please don't receive it that way. It is the exact opposite. It is the reality that Jesus loves you so much that He cares about screening out the lies Satan tells you. And He wants you just to listen to Him and believe Him.

Recently we were dealing with a beautiful couple. We spent many hours going over the basics we have just been considering. It became agonizingly clear to us that these people were living without great expectations. They were just living, grinding life out. They had received all kinds of advice and ideas from friends, relatives and others who told them, "Well, you've had enough. Why don't you just wrap this marriage up and forget it." Then God comes upon us and says, *"Don't let them get by with that. I've got a blueprint for both of them, and they are supposed to be together—now you put them together. Get them together. Get them to try it. Stop the lawyer."* That's what God does with us constantly. The man, as he received this from me, said, "Well, I understand that Book has a law against divorces, and if we break that law we are going to get in trouble, and we shouldn't do it that way."

And we reply, "No, you missed it completely; that isn't what it is all about. It is completely the reverse. The law says, 'Do this and you shall live.'" That's what Jesus says! Jesus is not the one who gives the law that destroys us. He lets the law be a breaking point for us. But it's Jesus reaching out, saying, *"Live this way and you will be at peace."* He does not say, "If you don't live this way, I'll clobber the living daylights out of you." This is what Satan says to people in church after church, home after home. He tells them, "You have done so much that you can never be forgiven." That's not true. God speaks it very clearly—*"Do this and you shall live."* He never says, "If you don't keep every single part of the law, I'll knock you so hard you won't know what happened, and I'll hound you to your grave." That's all devil-talk. The "accuser of the brethren" stands, as he did in the past, accusing people and throwing guilt upon them. And Jesus is standing right there in the midst of it all saying, *"No, no, the Lord your God is mighty and He is in the midst of you—He's here to save you. He is here to set you free—to make you new people—He is not here to clobber you."*

"God did not send his Son into the world to condemn it, but to save it" (John 3:17, TLB). Grasp this! The *positive* thrust of it all! This we have to grab! This is the area we must understand. Jesus is so clear in this. Whenever we get to the point where we say, "Well, I didn't do it quite right and I failed and I guess Jesus is going to be angry with me," at that moment we have bought the *lie,* and we have forgotten who Jesus is. Because Jesus condemns no man. He said, through Paul, "There is therefore now no condemnation for those who are in Christ Jesus"(Rom. 8:1). But people just don't believe it. Do you? Try to believe it in a new way. I call you to a new understanding of who Jesus *really* is. He is a great Friend, but even more, He is closer to you than your own hands and feet.

He is so powerful, you see. But people don't live in the expectation of Jesus actually being in them. We become brokenhearted when some people decide they will go along with the world's lies instead of the truth of God. It makes us hurt.

We must learn to keep our eyes on Jesus. The devil doesn't like this at all. He tries his level best to keep you looking elsewhere. He says, "After all, you're quite capable. You know how to handle things now. You don't have to bother God about these things." Then you're on your way. That detour sign comes up, and there you are—going away from God. I know you can relate to this. This is where most of us live—in the midst of confusion! We are learning to keep our eyes on Jesus. Jesus said this to us in a prophetic word, *"When you look at me, there is no way the devil can look at you, because he can't look in my direction."* Now get a picture of that.

We had a vision about this truth. We had a picture of us looking at Jesus. He was saying, "Come on, come. It's all set." He was looking right at us, and Old Slewfoot did not dare look in our direction, because he does not dare look in the direction of Jesus. He appears to us, hiding himself from Jesus—turning his back to us and going away from us. That is why Jesus said, "Get behind Me, Satan!" (Matt. 16:23). We believe we must learn to keep our eyes on Jesus and His promises—and the reality of His truths, for He is faithful. He has proved His love for us, so far and so magnificently, that it is hard to grasp. But *He* has done it. J.B. Phillips, in his beautiful *New Testament in Modern English,* speaks directly to this in his translation of this passage: "For thy sake we are killed all the day long; We were accounted as sheep for the slaughter. No, in all these things we win an overwhelming victory through him [Jesus] who has proved his love for us" (Rom. 8:36-37).

Mel Tari, an evangelist from Indonesia, deals with this so beautifully in a lot of the descriptions of miracles in his book *Gentle Breeze of Jesus.* Mel shares ten years of experience with the miracles God performs every single day. The vitality of it—the reality of it! Yet the Indonesian people are not struggling like we are. If these things would happen in America, we would have our video cameras and the press there to check everything out. We would do that because supernatural phenomena are so surprising to us. But the Indonesians just say, "Why, that's God. That's His normal, everyday thing." Mel says the reason the revival has not stopped in Indonesia is because the people haven't taken their eyes off of Jesus and put them on His miracles.

This really speaks to me. I think it is important for us to grasp this truth. We can expect miracles if we keep our eyes on Jesus. He will assure us with every word, every look, every attitude. He *will* assure us.

7
Living in Expectation
of What Jesus Will Do

I remember a story Mel Tari's wife tells to describe the first time she went to Timor, Indonesia. She wanted so much to be a part of this grand new experience of seeing people healed. She expected to find hospitals empty and no sickness anywhere. She found, to her surprise, that many people still went to hospitals because they just did not believe. They did not believe that Jesus could heal them. They saw other people being healed by Jesus, but they did not choose to be healed. Mrs. Tari reports that one day word came to their home that a little baby had been born with a deformed arm—no arm there at all—just a stub. Someone from the ministry teams was called and told to go out and pray for that family. So, one of the ladies quit her morning's work and went to the little village to take care of the situation. Mrs. Tari was very excited about this and anxious to see the power of Jesus restore that baby's limb. She waited, expecting the lady to break in at any time to report the startling news that the limb had been restored. The lady returned to her own home and began preparing the evening meal without speaking a word to Mrs. Tari. This was too much for Mel's American wife. She rushed over to the lady's home and asked, "What happened? Tell me all about it." The lady's calm reply was, "Oh, we found that the trouble wasn't with the baby, but with the grandfather who had been practicing sorcery. So, we dealt with him, and he's all taken care of. He's now a new creature in Christ. We'll go back another day and take care of the baby."

Jesus is always there. The sin of the grandfather was the cause of this little child's deformity. God took care of the cause of the deformity, then another time she would be able to return and see the baby healed. Jesus is there all the time. He's *here* all the time. But too many people do not live in such expectations! As a result, people grind their way through life hoping someone or something will change all this—because we just don't release His power as we should.

The other factor to remember in dealing with people during their agonizing times is that people don't live in the expectation that Jesus is going to do what He says He will do. Do you grasp what I'm saying? People may say, "Well, I didn't have enough faith, or perhaps one person in the room didn't have enough faith. The conditions were not quite right." We get all wrapped up in rationalizing why certain miracles do not occur, when the simple fact is that Jesus decided not to do it just then. It's easy to say that everytime we set it up, God has to move. That's not the way He works. God is in control; He is sovereign, and we are His submitted channels. The signs will indeed follow—but as He lets them follow. For it is God who creates the signs that follow those who believe. Can you see this?

Suddenly you are set free from the fear of failure in

praying for miracles of healing and the movement of Jesus to touch His hurting people. There is no need to feel, "What if I pray for this person, and he doesn't get well?" I've had many people say to me, "How do you dare pray for them? They might lose their faith." I struggled with this for years, but not any more. We anoint people for healing. Why not? God is in the business of setting men free. He goes about it as He chooses. He told us, His disciples, to do these works, and we're just going to do what He told us to do—and many, many times the miracles *do* happen. Every time we pray for healing of memories, we stand in awe of His power. Every time we anoint a person with oil for the healing of memories, I know what's happening. I know a miracle is taking place as I obey Jesus and touch the person with oil—something happens right then. We have plenty of evidence stacked up, and we could give literally hundreds of case histories of people who have been completely set free through the healing of memories. They cannot have any more pain from those memories. And if we meet them a few days later, they are looking at us with beautiful smiles on their faces.

I recently talked with a girl who was trying to commit suicide. She started believing Jesus after she got all the garbage out of her. She just gave it all to Jesus. He chucked it all away, and she began to believe Him and was baptized in the Holy Spirit. She started to smile. She was healed of her memories and her wounded spirit, and by Friday of that week, she was so full of the joy of the Lord you could hardly believe it. I said to her, "How are your memories?"

She answered, "Fascinating! The pain's all gone! I'm not haunted by my memories any more. I'm not controlled by my fears any more."

It is just so beautiful. Jesus *is* faithful. Please believe this. We must learn to live in the expectation that Jesus is going to do what He promises to do—for *He is faithful!*

8
Believing Jesus to Touch His People

Let's read several passages of Scripture from *The New Testament in Modern English* by J.B. Phillips. "All our persuading of men [and women], then, is with this solemn fear of God in our minds" (2 Cor. 5:11). (This is what I believe we are trying to do at Okontoe Fellowship.) "What we are is utterly plain to God—and I hope to your consciences as well. (No, we are not recommending ourselves to you again, but we can give you grounds for legitimate pride in us—if that is what you need to meet those who are so proud of the outward rather than the inward qualification.)" (2 Cor. 5:12-13). Paul is saying, "I've got a few degrees I can throw out if you are having trouble with that." Isn't that neat? I heard a man once say, "After the baptism in the Holy Spirit and being born again, you don't need to worry about college degrees. You all have a B.A.—born again."

"The very spring of our actions is the love of Christ," Paul continues. "We look at it like this: if one died for all men then, in a sense, they all died, and his purpose in dying for them is that their lives should now be no longer lived for themselves, but for him who died and rose again for them" (2 Cor. 5:14). Isn't that beautiful? "This means that our knowledge of men can no longer

43

be based on their outward lives (indeed, even though we knew Christ as a man we do not know him like that any longer). For if a man is in Christ he becomes a new person altogether—the past is finished and gone, everything has become fresh and new. All this is God's doing, for he has reconciled us to himself through Jesus Christ; and he has made us agents of the reconciliation. God was in Christ personally reconciling the world to himself—not counting their sins against them—and has commissioned us with the message of reconciliation. We are now Christ's ambassadors, as though God were appealing direct to you through us. As his personal representative we say [as we say again and again in counseling], 'Make your peace with God' " (2 Cor. 5:16-20). That's what we proclaim. "Come on, children, don't block His power from entering your life any more."

In his book, *How Did It All Begin?* (Logos, 1976), Harold Hill makes an important statement about "negative bias." He writes, "When you, by an act of your will, inject the bias, the negative energy, of unbelief into the human mind, it closes down your receptivity mechanism. You become a blockhead—blocked from God's best by your deliberate, willful negative bias."

Recently God brought this illustration to mind as we were talking to people who would understand. We said, "When you have a negative bias, it is as if you put a gate down on the circuit coming in. When that stops, you stop the inward flow of power." God's interpretation of that to me was, "When you do that, you allow the other power to be a part of your life, and you shut off the power of God to you by your negative bias." I've struggled to understand this. It is always a double circuit. If you cut yourself off from God, you say, "Welcome, Mr. Devil." There it is, whether we like it or not. It's that clear cut. If you don't proclaim Jesus and say, "Yes, I believe in Him" you are saying yes to Satan. Jesus said, "He who is not with Me is against Me" (Matt. 12:30).

Let us continue with the thoughts of Paul: "God caused Christ, who himself knew nothing of sin, actually to *be* sin for our sakes, so that in Christ we might be made good with the goodness of God. As cooperators with God himself we beg you, then, not to fail to use the grace of God" (2 Cor. 5:21-6:1, Phillips).

Isn't that powerful? So, in our counseling we plead with people, day after day. "Don't fail to use His grace. It's available. His grace is sufficient for you. It will take care of all your needs. Believe it!"

And people will say, "Well, I don't know. It's awfully hard. If you knew this man the way I know him. You just can't imagine all the things he's done to me."

I reply, "Try me. I've heard about all I can imagine of the cruel things people do to one another. But that doesn't matter, because God doesn't look at this any more. We are not concerned about the surface things you're talking about. We know you've had trouble. We know you've hated each other. We know you've struggled. That isn't what we're talking about. What we want to hear is, 'Do you believe *God* can do something about it? Come on, let's let Him do it! We're cooperators with God, and we'd love to show you that Jesus will do it for you, if you'd like to do it today.' " And that is where it is. That's the truth, I believe, that we're dealing with.

45

Another powerful passage from God's Word speaks to this as well: "To you, who were spiritually dead all the time that you drifted along on the stream of this world's ideas of living, and obeyed its unseen ruler (who is still operating in those who do not respond to the truth of God), to you Christ has given life! We all lived like that in the past, and followed the impulses and imaginations of our evil nature, being in fact under the wrath of God by nature, like everyone else"(Eph. 2:1-3, Phillips). Isn't that where you were? "But even though we were dead in our sins God, who is rich in mercy, because of the great love he had for us, gave us life together with Christ" (Eph. 2:4, Phillips).

He doesn't say, "Hey, I'll teach you how to live, then when you get to heaven you can talk to Jesus about it." He says, *I give you life; I give it to you in Jesus.* He doesn't send you out like sheep among wolves. He says, *"I'll go ahead of you. I'll be right there with you."* God gives us life—*with* Christ. Oh, that speaks to me! It takes all the fear out of my gut. That's what happened! I don't have that ache in my gut any more. I had that condition for years because I was always asking, "What if?" The "What ifs?" of life depart quickly when we hand over the controls to Jesus.

9

Cutting the Nerve of Instinctive Actions

"It is, remember, by grace and not by achievement that you are saved—and [he] has lifted us right out of the old life to take our place with him in Christ Jesus in the Heavens" (Eph. 2:5-6, Phillips). One foot on the earth and the other in heaven. We have a dual citizenship, but our real home is not this earth.

"Thus he shows for all time the tremendous generosity of the grace and kindness he has expressed toward us in Christ Jesus" (Eph. 2:7, Phillips). Do you think of the grace and generosity, and do you dwell on it? Do you raise your hands and praise Him for it? Are you excited because He does this for you? We tend to forget His generosity in the turmoil that swirls around us, don't we? And we begin to cry like the world. Then Jesus sits down and cries with us and says, *"Why do you weep? Why do you weep?"* We answer, "They've taken away my Lord, and I know not where they have laid Him." But Jesus says, *"Loved one, it is I. Touch me not—go tell the others!"*

You know, "It was nothing you could or did achieve—it was God's gift of grace which saved you. No one can pride himself upon earning the love of God. The fact is that what we are we owe to the hand of God

upon us" (Eph. 2:9, Phillips). Thank you, Jesus! Hallelujah! "For we are his workmanship, created in Christ
Jesus to do those good deeds which God planned for us
to do!" (Eph. 2:10, Phillips). That takes the "karma"
concept of Hinduism—good works (the how-to-earn-
the-grace-of-God)—right out and throws it where it
belongs—in the garbage can. And it puts the truth
where it belongs. God has already planned what we are
to do, and if we will just listen to Him and believe
Him—*accept Him* and receive Him by faith—it will all
happen! Now that's exciting.

So many people look at us and say, "How can you be
so optimistic about life? Here you are, still waiting for
God to open up a new ministry center for you."

I will answer, "You bet we are, and we're on the way.
It's going to come. There's money coming in for this
thing, and God has a plan He's working out. The next
thing you know, we're going to be in a new place. We
aren't sitting anxiously about cranking out our fears
and wondering how we are going to make it through
this thing! We're just blessing God that four families
can live in one house. Bending and blending, you know.
That's what He keeps telling us." But what is happening
is that we're learning to love one another as we've never
loved one another before, and God is blessing us, and
God is using that humble dwelling on a little old farm
near Annandale to bring His glory down upon people
who walk in and receive it! We stand in awe! And when
one person sits in the chair where we've been counseling
in our bedroom—a little office and bedroom—and
they start complaining that they can't comprehend all

this, I say, "Well, you're sitting in the seat where yesterday God made it clear to another person."*

You see, the reality of life, as Jesus moves among us, is just so great that we can't grasp it. But He has a plan for us, and when you start believing He has a plan for you, then things are going to take off. Then it's going to be fun. In anticipation of what He does, you will be thankful and eager, instead of saying, "Oh, I wonder what's going to happen next?"

Look at the following verses from the Phillips paraphrase: "You cannot, indeed, be a Christian at all unless you have something of his spirit in you" (Rom. 8:9). Look at the positive thrust of this passage. "If Christ does live within you his presence means that your sinful nature is dead, but your spirit becomes alive" (Rom. 8:10). Do you see this? Your spirit comes alive as Jesus lives within you—because of the "righteousness that He brings with Him." There it is again— His plan for our lives. "I said that our nature is 'dead' in the presence of Christ, and so it is, because of its sin. Nevertheless once the Spirit of him who raised Christ Jesus from the dead lives within you he will, by the same Spirit, bring to your whole being new strength and vitality" (Rom. 8:10-11).

That's the promise! That's what God says to us. Let the old man die. Don't try to keep him alive!

I once heard a person say, "Our marriage died seven

---

*This experience took place in 1976-77. Then in the fall of 1977 the present Okontoe Fellowship Ministry Center became a reality. Now five families and four young adults, believing Jesus still touches His people today, minister to thousands who come seeking help.

years ago, and I don't know whether I want to try to breathe life back into it."

I responded, "I've got news for you—Jesus isn't in the funeral business! He's in the resurrection business! If you begin believing this, you won't have to worry about the dead marriage, because you'll get a new marriage that will just blow you away. And you'll say, 'How did I miss all this before?' "

"So then, my brothers [and sisters], you can see that we have no particular reason to feel grateful to our sensual nature, or to live life on the level of the instincts" (Rom. 8:12, Phillips). That's what the world is receiving as the way to live today. The whole world teaches us to live on the level of our instincts and show gratitude to our sensual natures—gratify them! But not so Jesus. The Bible says, "Indeed that way of living leads to certain spiritual death" (Rom. 8:13, Phillips). You are guaranteed to die spiritually if you go that way, because your soul will head you right into hell fast. And before you know it, you'll be having instructions from the devil every day—such as, "Why don't you go out and kill yourself?" That's what is happening in this generation. Day by day we hear it. "But if on the other hand you cut the nerve of your instinctive actions by obeying the Spirit, you are on the way to real living" (Rom. 8:13, Phillips).

Our instinctive actions may be good in many instances. Our instinctive need to survive could keep us alive in an accident. *But*, the instinctive actions the world is teaching us to obey more often are destructive and *self-indulging.* Many authors today are teaching people to go *natural*—"*Do* what you *feel* like doing." Blow up and tell somebody off! It will make you feel better! The world says, "If you have a sex desire, satisfy it— whether it's with your own wife or someone else!" The world says, "Accept as natural the lust of the eye and learn to feel no guilt! Obey the call of your instincts and you'll be a free man or woman!"

But God's Word says exactly the opposite! See Matt. 5:22 and 5:38-39 about anger! Jesus equates anger with *murder*. He tells us to forget retaliation and start giving to others! Paul declares, "Walk by the Spirit, and you will not carry out the desire of the flesh. For the flesh sets its desire against the Spirit" (Gal. 5:16-17). Jesus says, "Every one who looks on a woman to lust for her has committed adultery with her already in his heart" (Matt. 5:28). This causes a warfare to ensue in our lives when we hear such conflicting ideas! Like Paul, we find ourselves caught, wanting in our hearts to do what God calls us to do and yet, at the same time, in our natural selves, we go on doing what is destructive! Paul said, "It is an agonizing situation, and who on earth can set me free from the clutches of my own sinful nature?" (Rom. 7:24, Phillips). The answer Paul discovered is the answer we all need to hear!

"If . . . you cut the nerve of your instinctive actions by obeying the Spirit, you are on the way to real living" (Rom. 8:13, Phillips).

Cutting the nerves of our instinctive actions is God's answer to the warfare in mankind today. And this is done only by obeying the promptings of the Holy Spirit, which lead us to God's perfect life here on earth and into eternity! That life is *real*—not full of illusions ending in tragedies we see daily! This is not *frustrating*—for the Spirit teaches us and shows us the better way wherein we do find true satisfaction and escape the consequences of sin! When a nerve is cut in your wrist, the hand is no longer able to function. When the nerves in your elbow and shoulder are cut, what happens? The arm becomes useless! It cannot even react to threats to your body!

So, think of your arm as hanging loosely, unable to move or react when someone approaches you in anger and strikes you! You can't strike back at him, because your arm is useless! You can't act instinctively and retaliate! So you may have to do what Jesus told you to do, "Whoever slaps you on your right cheek, turn to him the other also!" (Matt. 5:39).

Even so is God's plan for us as we start walking in the Spirit! As we allow our nerves of instinctive action to be cut—by obeying the promptings of the Holy Spirit—we will find what Jesus tells us to do to be utterly *real* and *deeply life changing!*

I experienced this one night at the end of a teaching I had given at a large meeting in St. Paul, Minnesota. At the end of the meeting many people came up to talk with me. As I stood there steaming from the exertion of speaking under the Holy Spirit's anointing, a woman approached me and very shortly said, "I don't see how you can stand here and say God guides you the way you say, when I have asked Him to help me lose weight and He didn't!"

How would you reply? Instinctively I could have

said, "Well, fat lady, if you would just exercise some will power and push away the food, you would find God cooperating with you, and you would lose weight." Or, I could have risen to defend my God by proving that I have evidence piled up a mile high to show God constantly does guide me! Both of these would be instinctive actions, and both would *not* have been from God—nor would they have helped the dear lady!

As I was rearing up—*instinctively*—to defend my God, the Holy Spirit spoke clearly to me! He said simply, *"Love her!"* And because I was wanting to have the nerves of my instinctive actions cut, I obeyed the Spirit! I reached out and touched her on the cheek and softly asked, "Loved one, what really is the matter?" I put my arm around her husband standing there, and they both were touched by the Holy Spirit operative in my arms—and began to melt before me! He had lost his job—they had to sell their home, and they were under great stress and, in the process, they had overeaten!

Because I allowed the nerves of my instinctive actions to be cut by obeying the promptings of the Holy Spirit, God touched those two people, and they were helped as they came for counseling later on, and God's plans for them began opening up! The *"real living"* started becoming a reality for them and for *me,* too!

PART II

The Gifts of the Spirit

Rev. Bill Barr, Jr.

10
How We Use the Gifts of the Spirit in Counseling

How do we use the gifts of the Spirit in ministering through counseling? To begin, let us turn to 1 Cor. 2:10 and the verses following. Paul has just described to the Corinthians that he did not come to them with words of men's wisdom, but he came to them demonstrating the power of the Holy Spirit. So, their faith could not rest on the words of men but on the power of God. We have found in counseling situations that people need to meet Jesus and to experience the power of God through the Holy Spirit. One of the ways God does this is through the gifts of the Holy Spirit. He touches people's lives. He reveals their needs, then ministers to their needs by His Spirit!

As we are agents of this ministering, it's important to see the divine perspective. In verse 10 it becomes clearer: God has revealed to us, through the Holy Spirit, "all that God has prepared for those who love Him." God reveals these things in order for His people to minister.

For the Spirit searches everything, even the depths of God. For what person knows a man's thoughts except the spirit of the man which is in him? So also no one comprehends the thoughts of God except the Spirit of God. Now we have received not the spirit of the world, but the Spirit which is from God, that we might understand the gifts bestowed on us by God. And we impart this in words not taught by human wisdom but taught by the Spirit, interpreting spiritual truths to those who possess the Spirit. The unspiritual man does not receive the gifts of the Spirit of God, for they are folly to him, and he is not able to understand them because they are spiritually discerned. The spiritual man judges all things, but is himself to be judged by no one. 'For who has known the mind of the Lord so as to instruct him?' But we have the mind of Christ. (1 Cor. 2:10-16, RSV)

In this framework, counseling in the Spirit takes its form. The Holy Spirit has access to the thoughts of God as well as to the thoughts and motivations of men. As we trust Him and lean on Him, He will reveal to us the mind of Jesus Christ, in order to minister to the spiritual man. It's important to see this as we begin to discuss the gifts of the Spirit.

Let's examine 1 Cor. 12 to see what the gifts of the Spirit are and to identify them briefly, and then we will discuss how God uses them in the counseling process.

Now there are varieties of gifts, but the same Spirit; and there are varieties of service, but the same Lord; and there are varieties of working, but it is the same God who inspires them all in every one. To each is given the manifestation of the Spirit for the common good. To one is given through the Spirit the utterance of wisdom, and to another the utterance of knowledge according to the same Spirit, to another faith by the same Spirit, to another gifts of healing by the one Spirit, to another the working of miracles, to another prophecy, to another the ability to distinguish between spirits [or the discernment of spirits], to another various kinds of tongues, to another the interpretation of tongues. All these are inspired by one and the same Spirit, who apportions to each one individually as he wills. (1 Cor. 12:4-11, RSV)

This is a very familiar passage to all of us, and yet most of the time, we don't think about the gifts of the Spirit in the context of the counseling situation. Most of the time we have a reference to the gifts in the Body, in a prayer meeting or a worship service of some sort. Or somebody will get up and give a prophecy as a word from the Lord. Somebody will bring forth a message in tongues and the interpretation. Somebody will pray for a person to be healed. There will be an anointing in this way. There will be a word of knowledge or a word of wisdom. These are designed for the common good of the people of God—to minister in the body, very definitely. But we have found that they are also designed by God to be channels into our daily lives, to give us His wisdom, His knowledge, His power, His healing—to minister to those in need. We believe God wants to communicate with us, as His people, to show us His way and to help us walk in His way—as well as to minister to those in need. So, we need to expect God to utilize us, through the gifts of the Holy Spirit, to reach into the body of Christ and into the world.

It's really exciting when you get started in this whole thing. You begin to see God move and reveal His Word and His will to people. They are profoundly touched by His Word—cut to the very quick and healed to the very quick—by God himself. And it's exciting to sit there and watch Him do it! To be the mouthpiece for His Word and love is really beautiful!

Many times, after we have had a time to counsel people and let the Lord bring their needs to the surface, and He begins to reach into their lives, as we begin to pray for them, the Lord speaks to them in a word of prophecy. It goes so deep, right down to the very root of their lives. Another pastor and I were counseling a couple who were living together without benefit of marriage. They had just come to the Lord. They had a little baby out of wedlock; the man was black and the woman was white. Their lives were in quite a mess. But the Lord was beginning to give them light. They had been convicted that they needed to get married. They wanted to get their lives straightened out, and they came to the pastor and said, "We would like to get married; would you please do it?"

The pastor looked at them, gulped, and said, "Hey, wait a minute!" So there we were. We sat down and shared and ministered to them so that they could be set free from the things that were binding them—that were ruining their lives. We had a blessed time of sharing with them. We prayed and the Lord touched them in a powerful way. He had already revealed their needs, and they had been very candid in sharing their backgrounds and their desire for the Lord to touch them. Then the Lord spoke in a word for the woman first. He told her that He loved her and that He loved her so much that He had died for her—and that she was His very own. He wanted her to know that. It was the sword of the spirit of love going right into her heart—to break away the bondage and the rejection and the fear and hurt that were there. She just melted. Then the Lord touched the man in the same way. They were transformed in our very presence. They were touched by the very presence of the Lord. Not by our own wise words—but by the Lord himself. They have never been the same since. Things are going to be right. They are married, and the Lord is working things out in their lives. Praise God! He does all things well.

Well, how do we utilize the gifts of the Spirit in counseling? The above experience is one way. We did not realize all the ways the Lord was going to use us in the counseling ministry until He took us into the midst of it. He began to send people to us who didn't know the Lord—or who had known the Lord and were even baptized in the Spirit—who had desperate needs. Needs for deliverance, for inner healing, for repentance and forgiveness, for reconciliation with loved ones, for healing of broken families, broken hearts, and rebellious kids—people who had come out of the "pit," literally smelling and reeking of hell! We said, "Lord, what do you want to do for them? We don't know how to take care of their needs. Here we are, Lord, we just happen to be some of your people here. What do you want to do?"

And He began to show us. In fact, we hadn't even received many of the gifts of the Spirit in our Christian community at Okontoe Camp—until people came to us for ministry. People came to the camp and said, "I'm hurting! Please pray for me."

We would gulp and say, "OK, Lord, what do you want us to do for them?" Then He began to speak—in prophecies, in words of knowledge. He began to heal people and deliver them. The process developed as He moved. We had no idea how to do it. But He began to do it and began to show us that as He moves, people are changed. Lives are touched. So we were blessed because we began to experience the gifts of the Spirit as other people came to us with their needs.

I know we had spent years waiting on the Lord. "Lord, please speak to us. Please speak to us." It was like Heaven had become brass. Not a word came through. We waited and waited. We said, "Well, I guess the Lord just doesn't care. He doesn't want to speak to us." But that was not true. He wanted to demonstrate to us why He had given the gifts—for the common good—to minister to the needs of people. Not just for our own vainglory, but to bless us. He wanted to use us, too.

I'll never forget the first time I ever received a prophecy. A family had brought a blind girl to our camp one fall just as we were closing the camp. She had developed blindness from diabetes and glaucoma, and the doctors had punctured one of her eyeballs to relieve the pressure. She was a very miserable young woman, very bitter and hurt, feeling rejected and hateful. The camp was basically closed, but some of the staff were still there. Some friends of ours had brought this person up for ministry. They said, "We don't know what the Lord wants to do, but we know that the couple is here for a reason—for the Lord to touch them."

We said, "OK, we'll ask the Lord." So, we had a day of prayer and fasting and said, "Lord, what do you want to do?" We prayed in different shifts, and I was given the blessing of praying with a dear sister in the Lord, Mildred Bent. She was about seventy years old at the time, a real warrior for the Lord and a channel of God's Word. We went out by the lake and sat there praying in the afternoon, asking the Lord what He wanted to do. "Do you want to heal her eyes? Do you want to heal her soul? What do you want to do, Lord?" Then the Lord spoke in a prophecy to Mildred. *"I desire to wash the windows of her soul—and to make her whole. But in order for her to receive that, she needs to forgive her husband and relinquish the burdens she's carrying to me."*

That was a blessing. It was also an awesome thing, for we had never prayed for anybody like that before. We did not know what to do or how to do it. Mildred said, "Lord, that is a pretty awesome thing. Would you please give us a confirmation? And please use Bill so that I don't get in the way."

I had never received a prophecy in my life. Yet she said, "Lord, use Bill." So I gulped and said, "OK, Lord, I'm willing if you are willing." I yielded my spirit to the Lord—and then simply waited. He gave me prophecy in a way that I have never experienced since. It was like a little ticker tape—tiny words that went right across my mind. I could see them running from one side of my mind to the other, and I could easily read the words right off the "tape." He confirmed it right there. He said, *"Yes, I do desire to heal her and to make her whole."*

Well, Mildred and I kept our mouths shut! That evening we got together and had a fellowship meeting and a time of ministry. As we sat down to worship the Lord, the Holy Spirit fell on us in a way we could never have imagined. We had never experienced the Lord in that way. It was like the air was heavy with the Spirit of God. It was breathtaking! We could hardly breathe, and we could not speak for we did not dare speak! It was a holy moment, and we were simply dumbfounded! Then a sister in the Lord began to prophesy, and I received another prophecy, the second one of my life. They were words of blessing that expressed the Lord's desire to heal us and to move upon us and to minister to our needs! Then a "rookie in the Lord" (one of the young men who had come for ministry that summer when he did not know the Lord—then he found Him and was baptized in the Spirit), received his first prophecy. He was a beautiful Catholic brother who had changed our attitude about Catholics. The Lord had done a beautiful work in our lives through him! He turned to the lady and gave this prophecy: "Jesus wants to make you whole and to heal your eyes and your heart—but you must repent and be healed in your relationship with your husband!" The Lord was doing something that day. The Word was going out that the Lord was going to do a work in this lady's life, whether we liked it or not, whether we were willing or not! He wanted to do the work. He had prophesied through three different people that He wanted to do this work. We had not told the "rookie" that the Lord had spoken to Mildred and me. We had not told anybody. We were just going to see how the Lord led in that meeting that night. Well, He led and took off running, and we all were trying to catch up!

When the Lord says something like that, what do you do? You have to put feet on your faith and go out and do something about it. So, we got up and stood around this woman, in fear and trembling, for we did not know what the Lord was going to do. We knew what He *wanted* to do, but we did not know He was going to do it through us! We prayed and agreed and bound up the spirit of diabetes and commanded it to loose her body. We called her to repentance and forgiveness and healing with her husband. She turned to him and asked for his forgiveness. He forgave her, and he asked her forgiveness—and life began to pour into them!

At that time, the girl, who had received the first prophecy that evening, grew upset and ran out of the room. Then her husband went charging out of the room, too—trying to see what was wrong. It so happened that she was frustrated and felt like the Lord had shut her off! She could not figure out why. Later, she realized the Lord was passing the torch! Those two friends had been used as catalysts in our community to open hearts to receive words from the Lord. The Lord had just turned off that "spigot" that night and turned on others, so that we would know He was transferring the gifts to our community!

We had prayed and nothing seemed to be happening, so we asked, "Lord, is there anything in our hearts that blocks this healing?" Then we repented of our unbelief and asked the Lord to unite us in faith. I walked out of the room to see what was happening to the couple who had left. While I was gone, all of a sudden there was tremendous whooping and hollering from people who were praising the Lord! We heard them jumping up and down with shouts of joy and rejoicing! The blind lady had begun to see light! Somebody had walked between her and a light, and she had seen the shadow! She was beginning to see! We had never had anything like this happen before, and we were just praising the Lord for what He was doing! We all went back into the room and had a good "Hallelujah breakdown" and then went to bed!

The next morning, the brother who had brought these people for ministry, Lowell Mattson, had gone out on our lake and was paddling around in a canoe waiting on the Lord. The Lord had taken him over to our gravel pit, prostrated him on the ground, and touched his life in a profound way! At the same time, God healed his neck of a whiplash accident! Lowell could hardly turn his neck before that moment, and when he came in that morning he could almost turn it around completely—like an owl!! God was clearly doing something great in his life, too! (Note: Lowell and Nancy Mattson and their children are now missionaries in Nome, Alaska, where they are being vitally used to give the good news to Indians and Eskimos through Radio Station KICY.)

Lowell said, "Something is happening to the blind lady today! Her one eye that was totally black is regaining its color! The Lord is healing the iris of her eye!" He reported that the couple had spent the whole night out in front of their fire sharing and talking to each other for the first time in years. The Lord had started the work! We were blessed and so we continued praising the Lord. Someone received the baptism in the Holy Spirit that next day—and then everyone went home!!

This particular lady lost her healing, much to our heartbreak and disappointment, as she walked back into her environment! She had been programed to think in the ways of the world. To think blindness. To think handicap. Spiritually she was still bound. We did not know, at that time, how to minister further to her. The Lord did not really lead us to that, either. He had touched her, and she knew it, but she rejected it! Our God had done a work in her, and He had done a work in our hearts, too. He had opened the door for ministry in our lives in a way we had never dreamed was possible. He had turned the Mattsons' lives around and was beginning to lead them to the mission field, where they now serve! He had given Joe Manahan a prophecy and initiated him into a whole new walk in the Spirit! He had used another couple beautifully to transfer the gifts of the Spirit to our community. The ministry in the Spirit began in my life and the blessing of the Lord has come in a beautiful way ever since. Praise the Lord! God is so good!

As people come to you with their needs, *expect* God to speak through you. Expect Him to minister, and He will do the work! Then it is His job to take care of the people as they go away. Our responsibility is to be channels of His love, not to try and justify what we are doing. Rather, we are to proclaim what the Lord wants to do and how He lives in us.

11

The Gifts—Evidence of Authority to Minister

Let's look for a minute in the Word again and see what basis the Lord has given to us to minister in this way. In Luke 10, describing the authority we have as believers, Jesus shares with His disciples that because they believed and were children of God, they had authority to minister! Jesus had sent the disciples out, seventy of them, as He had sent the twelve once before. Jesus sent them out, two by two, to minister the gospel. The Matthew account is very specific in its description of the authority He gave them. "He . . . gave them authority over unclean spirits, to cast them out, and to heal every disease and every infirmity" (Matt. 10:1, RSV). In verses 6 to 8, Jesus told them, "Go . . . to the lost sheep of the house of Israel. And preach as you go, saying, 'The kingdom of heaven is at hand.' Heal the sick, raise the dead, cleanse lepers, cast out demons. You received without paying, give without pay" (RSV). In the *New American Standard Bible,* we read, "Freely you have received, freely give" (Matt. 10:8). The Gospel of Luke reports that after sending out the seventy in the same way, they came back "with joy, saying, 'Lord, even the demons are subject to us in your name!' And he said to them, 'I saw Satan fall like lightning from heaven.

Behold, I have given you authority to tread upon serpents and scorpions, and over all the power of the enemy; and nothing shall hurt you'"(Luke 10:17, RSV).

When these verses came to us, God began to open doors for ministry that we had not anticipated. He began to demonstrate to us that He had given us authority over all the power of the enemy, and because He had given it to us, we were to use it! Otherwise, it would have no value. That gift would have no value at all if we didn't utilize it. If we didn't begin to walk in that authority. Jesus was tested in His authority after His baptism in the Jordan and His baptism in the Spirit. Satan tested Him to see whether He would stand in His authority or relinquish it to the devil. We found we had the same testing opportunity, but as we began to stand firm and walk in the power of the Spirit, Satan began to back away. As he did with Jesus, "he departed from Him until an opportune time." Directly following that testing time, Jesus went boldly in the power of the Spirit and began to minister. The Lord has done the same thing in our lives, and He is doing the same in your lives, so you will have the authority to minister to people who are greatly in need. So Jesus can heal the sick, raise the dead, cleanse the lepers, and cast out demons. That's still the work of Jesus in the world today! "He who believes and is baptized will be saved; but he who does not believe will be condemned. And these signs will accompany those who believe: in my name they will cast out demons; they will speak in new tongues; they will pick up serpents, and if they drink any deadly thing, it will not hurt them; they will lay their hands on the sick, and they will recover" (Mark 16:16-18, RSV).

Authority to minister! Isn't that it? The signs that follow often bring people to belief and confirm God's love for them. Praise the Lord! So we *have* authority because Jesus has granted it unto us, and we need to begin to use it! The world is crying out in its hunger to feel the touch of the Lord and the power of God. The world is desperately in need of receiving what we have within our grasp. That's why the Lord is doing the work! Once we begin to recognize what we have is a priceless treasure that millions of people are needing and wanting, then we have the freedom to go and share it. We need to open our hearts! Let the Lord use you, and you will be amazed at what happens!

So the gifts of the Spirit are evidence of authority to minister. What are these gifts? How do we use them? How do they function in a counseling situation? One of the things we learned a long time ago was that when Jesus does the work, He goes beyond the wisdom of men. In fact, many times He has to put aside the wisdom of men, in order for us to receive anything from Him.

The Lord spoke to me one day through a brother in the Lord. Jesus said, *"I want you to put away the philosophies of men and feed on My Word. Let My Word permeate your heart so that you may be my vessel."* I thought I had gotten rid of all those things. Well, the rest of them went out the window that day!

I said, "Lord, I want to be yours!" He had to cleanse my mind so that it would be pure and open to the voice of the Lord and the power of God, in order to minister.

Otherwise, we would be sitting here trying to figure out ways to patch up people by the wisdom of men. I'm not putting that down, but it is not adequate for today's problems. The Holy Spirit gives us the power, through the gifts of the Spirit, to reach conclusions that no man can reach. We need to recognize this, and then we need to go on. We began to find that as we prayed, we would ask the Lord, "What is the situation here? What is the need?" Then He would begin to speak through words of wisdom, knowledge, and prophecy and often through questions in our hearts. He would say, *"Ask this question: 'What happened to you when you were six years old? Is there a particular problem in your life relating to that period of your life?'"* Often the counselee would, in great surprise, wonder how we knew about that time in her life.

We would reply, "We didn't know. The Lord just asked us to ask you that question." That's how the word of knowledge begins to function! We would begin to ask God, "Does this person have a curse on them? Yes or no, Lord, we want to know; we really need a confirmation of this."

The Lord would say, *"Yes, they have a curse. Break it right now! I want to break it with you, because I hate to see them in bondage."* (This would come through the gift of prophecy.) Then we would see Him set them free and gloriously give them new life.

God says, "If any of you lacks wisdom, let him ask God, who gives to all men generously and without reproaching, and it will be given to him. But let him ask in faith, with no doubting, for he who doubts is like a wave of the sea that is driven and tossed by the wind. For that person must not suppose that a double-minded man, unstable in all his ways, will receive anything from the Lord" (James 1:5-8, RSV). We have learned that we need to ask the Lord.

We always pray when we begin a counseling session, "Lord, please grant us the gifts of the Spirit to minister." For some crazy reason, we forgot to pray on one particular day, and we could not figure out why we were not getting a breakthrough. This particular person was hiding his needs and camouflaging many hurts. Dad left the room for a minute for a break, and he prayed, "Lord, what's going on? How come we're not getting a breakthrough? Why aren't we receiving your gifts to minister to him?"

The Lord answered, *"You didn't ask me! You have not because you ask not!"*

Dad said, "Oh, sorry, Lord! Now I'm asking!" Then we got through, and the Lord began to move into this person's life and reveal the areas of his need. The man was not consciously aware of his needs! He had crammed them down into his subconscious so far that the hurts were not evident! As far as he was concerned, they were under control, but they were still there and actually controlling and ruling his life. This person was a minister who had a strange disease that was destroying his throat, so he could barely talk. He had been in an accident out in the woods and a tree had fallen on him, severely injuring his neck. There were strange kinds of aberrations in his life, and we said, "Lord, there has to be a reason for these! No man just goes along and has his voice taken away and his neck injured and all these strange things—when he is a man of God who is called to preach the gospel!" Then the Lord showed us there were areas of his life where he was in bondage and that Satan had controlled him through those things. We prayed for him and asked the Lord to heal him.

This man went away speaking in a halting, but improved, manner. His wife writes that he has improved but he is still not entirely whole. God continues to deal with him as he believes more in God's answers and methods than his own limited expectations.

12

Words of Wisdom, Words of Knowledge

The word of wisdom is God's supernatural wisdom that we ask for to be able to deal with particular problems. The word of knowledge is supernatural revelation from God, not man's knowledge nor man's wisdom. Yet these gifts function in such a simple way that many times we miss them. I remember when a friend of mine was sharing with me one day last summer; he said the Lord had revealed something to him. It was during a time when he was struggling with people not experiencing victory in their lives when they prayed. He realized it's all so simple—all you have to do is believe God and do it. And people kept saying, "We just can't! There's something wrong."

Then the Lord said, *"Don't be so harsh on this brother. Remember, I have given you the gift of faith, so you can believe. Other people must ask for this gift of faith, too."* It was happening so "supernaturally" natural in his life that he didn't realize it was a gift from God. The Lord had just placed it in his heart, and it was clear to him. Yes, if I believe that, it will happen. Hence, he was given the capacity to believe and things were happening. The Lord was answering his requests because of the faith that God had placed within his heart.

That's the way it happens! A lot of times we discover that the Lord is utilizing a gift in our lives, and we didn't even know it. But that's beautiful, because then we don't climb the wall trying to find that which is already there. It's a gift of the Spirit. It's manifesting itself from within us in a gentle way—words of knowledge, for example, will just come as thoughts in our minds.

I was walking along one time with a fellow who came to our camp, and the Lord told me he was a homosexual. I said, "Oh, come on!" In my mind, his homosexuality was clearly seen. I said, "Now wait a minute, Lord, what am I going to do with this now? That's kind of heavy. This man didn't even ask for ministry or anything. Lord, what do you want me to do?" I didn't know what to do with it, so I just "sat on it." Later, this man wrote a letter to my sister, as he had been a friend of hers years before, and shared the burden in his heart—that he was a homosexual and would like the Lord to do something about it. The Lord had confirmed that word of knowledge!

Another time the same thing happened. Bill Morel, my brother-in-law, and I were sitting down to counsel a young man, a teen-ager. Just as we were sitting down, the Lord told Bill that this youth was a homosexual. Bill said, "Lord, what are we going to do with that?" Well, the Lord worked it out in that session. The youth shared all the different hurts in his life and then said, "There's one area that I just can't tell you about. It's just too terrible."

We responded, "We can ask the Lord what it is, and He will tell us."

"Yes, I know, and He probably already has!"

Then Bill said, "Yes, He already has. Why don't *you* now tell us about it?" He then felt free to share it all, and he admitted that he was a homosexual and wanted God to help him. The Lord ministered to him. You see, God revealed that word of knowledge, not for our own good but for the good of that youth, so He could minister to him and set him free. If God had not revealed that knowledge, the boy would not have been able to share it.

The word of knowledge is designed as a means of ministry. A lot of times we will be going along and the Lord will say, *"Ask them if they had a premarital relationship."* Then we hear ourselves asking these nice, upstanding, Spirit-filled Christian people if they had had premarital relationships. It is a risky business—yet, when the Lord is doing it, it is worthwhile, and you can ask the most audacious questions with point-blank honesty and boldness. They will respond to the love of Jesus they sense and say, "Yes. We never knew it was wrong." The Lord wants to clean the decks, and He wants to go into every part of people's lives to reveal their needs and set them free.

If the Lord reveals a word of knowledge through you, ask for the gift of wisdom to know how to use it. The gift of wisdom functions to give you wisdom on how to minister. You will be evaluating a particular situation, for example, and suddenly the Lord will say, *"This really makes sense. This is the answer for his life."* Your mind will just go "click." A lot of times we will receive a word of wisdom and not even know it happened. But it suddenly becomes clear that "Yes, this is the right thing!" God's wisdom comes to bear on that situation.

Jesus, in His ministry, operated with the gifts every day. The gift of the word of knowledge functioned every time the Pharisees started questioning Jesus. Remember? When He was sitting in a house and the determined friends of a paralytic tore the roof off and lowered him before Jesus, Jesus said, "Your sins are forgiven!" The Pharisees started mumbling among themselves, "Only God can forgive sins." Jesus knew what they were saying even before they said it. That was a word of knowledge. Then Jesus, replying to their mumbled protests, asked, "Is it easier for me to say, 'Your sins are forgiven you' or 'take up your bed and walk?' " Then He said to the man, "Take up your bed and walk." The man obeyed and went away totally healed. Jesus was expressing His divine nature and power, so they could believe in Him.

Another time someone came up to Him and said, "Is it right to give money to Caesar?"

How did Jesus answer? "Do you have a coin?" Jesus wasn't on the spot. The one asking was. "Do you have a coin?" This was a word of wisdom. His Father gave Him wisdom right there. "Whose face is on that coin?"

"Caesar's."

"Well, give what is due to Caesar to Caesar, and give what is due to God to God." A word of wisdom. That was God's wisdom to deal with a nitty-gritty situation in a very simple way. Through that word of wisdom, Jesus knew exactly the intention of that man and turned a potentially dangerous trap into an eternal truth we still grasp.

That is how it happens in our counseling situations. The Lord will just break through, in a very simple way, and show us the answer. It will clearly make sense. Not just logical sense in the mind—but God's sense—as you have the mind of Christ.

One day in a prophecy, Jesus told us, *"I have never forgotten anything since the beginning of time. I know all the future, and I hold the present in my hands."* So if there is anything we need to know, He has the knowledge. He has never forgotten anything since the beginning of time—He knows everything! That's hard for us to conceive of, because we forget most things and remember only a portion of what takes place in our lives. But God has access to His total memory bank from all time. He knows everything that has happened to anybody in the universe. He is the one who is able to do a work in their lives. We are not trying to find wisdom from Satan or trying to be clairvoyant or anything like that. We are seeking the face of the Lord and asking Him to bring His life into the people's lives before us. We ask for knowledge, not for our sakes, but for theirs. Wisdom for their lives—for power to touch them, to change them, to minister to their needs.

13
Discernment of Spirits

You may be acquainted with the gift of discernment of spirits. You may have even received this gift, depending on how you have moved with the Holy Spirit. It is the supernatural capacity, by God's Holy Spirit, to discern (to know, to understand) whether we are dealing with a human spirit, a demonic spirit, or God's Holy Spirit. In counseling situations this gift is extremely important!

As we were dealing with a woman recently, she immediately began to debate with us about biblical issues. She came to ask theological questions, which hardly ever happens in counseling. The Lord told me she had a "religious spirit" that was controlling her. We could not get through to her for a while. Finally I told her I realized she needed to belong to a fellowship where she could grow in love and have some people stand with her in belief. I encouraged her to go to a Women's Aglow Bible study. My wife's Bible study was based on the women of the Bible and their ministries. I invited this lady to attend, because I knew the women in that group would be able to help her. These women were mature in the Lord and about her age. I felt they could reach into her life. I told my wife, before this lady attended her

Bible study, "I believe this woman has a 'religious spirit,' and she is liable to debate you in the study time. We really need to pray before she comes and bind that spirit." I went charging off to a meeting early that morning and forgot to pray with my wife to that end.

My wife did not forget to pray, and the hostess and my wife agreed together and bound that spirit and had a wonderful experience with her! The Lord clearly was touching her! Then that same lady was in a teaching that evening when I was sharing with a college charismatic fellowship, and it was no hassle at all! She was open, and she received what the Lord had to say. The Lord is good. I never had to tell her that she had a "religious spirit." I simply utilized that discernment and prayed for her.

It's important to know whether you are talking to a demon or a person! You do not want to minister to a silly demon! You want to get rid of it! It's important to know what is going on! If someone gets a prophecy, you need to know whether it's from the Lord or just from someone's flesh. The Lord has provided this gift of discernment of spirits as a vehicle of ministry and to provide checks and balances within the ministries. He has done this so His will can be accomplished! So expect God to reveal these things to you. The Lord has revealed many things to us through this particular gift. You will find a check in your spirit sometimes, and you will know God is guiding you and protecting you from error.

The first time we were ever involved in deliverance of people from demonic forces, friends experienced in deliverance were ministering with us. They were at our camp teaching and sharing with us. A friend of ours from a church my dad had served in Ohio was working with us that summer. He wanted to receive the baptism of the Holy Spirit, so we got together in a prayer meeting that night and said, "Let's pray with you for this baptism of the Spirit." He sat on the "hot seat," and we prayed for him. He seemed to receive his prayer language, but as he was going along speaking strangely, suddenly everybody in the room started to cringe inside! We had not run into this kind of thing before. Usually when someone gets their prayer language, there is real rejoicing and praise. That night as we tried to praise the Lord, we said, "Wait a minute! Something is not right here!" There was a check in our spirits! Those standing around him became aware that the language was like a witch doctor's chant or an Indian medicine man's chant! It was clearly not from the Lord at all! We said, "Lord, what's going on here? We want to know what's happening in this man's life." Dear Mildred Bent was sitting there, and the Lord revealed to her that a particular spirit was controlling him, and so we began to pray and rebuke that spirit in Jesus' name. We had about a three-hour deliverance session—in a very strange way!

We learned so much that night that we never have regretted those three hours! We learned we had authority in the amazing name of Jesus! As we saw this man writhing on the floor, talking to us in strange ways, we could see the demons controlling his body. We finally saw or discerned who Satan was and who the demons were, and that they were actually different than the person himself. We discovered we could get rid of those demons in the name of Jesus, because we had authority in that name and in the power of the blood of Jesus. At one point, one of us said to a stubborn demon, "We are now going to immerse this man in a barrel of the blood of Jesus!" This was totally new vocabulary for us—but I tell you at that moment that demon squirmed and squealed and cried out, "No, no, no, anything but that! Don't put me in the blood of Jesus! No! No!" Then he immediately released the man and the man was free! The physical appearance of that man started to change, and within two days the radiance of Jesus began to beam from him. He began to smile, when before he had nothing but fearful, sad features all over his face!

Jesus is Lord, and He wants us to function with His love! This particular night discernment was an important tool for protecting the Body and protecting that man from deception! If we had not had discernment that something was wrong, he would not have received what he wanted. The next day we prayed he would receive the fullness of the Spirit with his tongue from God! We waited a day before we got together with him, so he would have a chance to recuperate and get his heart in the right place. That day he received a beautiful prayer language as he praised the Lord for baptizing him in the Spirit and for setting him free from demons!

Another young man was waiting for the baptism of the Spirit, in the room with us as we were battling to deliver his close friend. He waited for three hours, flabbergasted at what was happening to his friend. He was going to be next in the chair. As he sat there, his eyes bugged out—he was terrified! Yet he said, "I want it,

Lord! I want all you have got for me, Father—right now! Please give it to me! Please baptize me with your Spirit!" Instantly, he got his prayer language—so fast we were amazed! He was sitting there speaking in his new tongue, rebuking the devil and standing firm in the Lord! He was so far up spiritually that as he took off the next day for Ohio, he drove straight through, about seventeen hours, without rest. He went into his prayer group and turned the whole place upside down. He knew what the Lord had done for his friend, and he knew he wanted what the Lord was going to give him to deal with the enemy. So, in the midst of the battle, he saw the mighty power of God and he wanted all that God would give him!

14
Prophecy—
God Speaking to His People Today

The gift of prophecy is used very frequently in counseling. I would say that in most counseling sessions, the Lord speaks to His people. It's part of His healing process. He desires to communicate to them, to reveal his love and His power and to touch their lives.

Dad and I were ministering to another pastor who was new in the community. He had come several times with people who needed counseling. He had sat with us in a few sessions and had assisted in the counseling process. He was really blessed with what he saw the Lord doing. His wife had been touched by a friend, who had been through one of our training sessions for counseling in the Spirit. She was leading a Women's Aglow Bible study, and this pastor's wife had attended. During that study the Lord moved upon her to deliver this pastor's wife from a spirit of rejection and some other things. She was gloriously set free, and she began asking her husband, "When are you going to get set free? You need some of this counsel and ministry too!"

He came and because he was really open, having seen what the Lord had done with his own congregation and now his wife, he finally said, "I guess it's my turn! I'd better come and get some things cleared up." The Lord was so good that day! We just sat down and started praying, before we could even start counseling, the Lord spoke to that pastor in a comforting prophecy! He touched him and moved upon him and ministered to him. Then, after all that, we started to counsel, but the Lord had already done most of the work! It was wonderful to see how He just laid it all out and set that man free. He is a beautiful brother in the Lord, and the Lord is using him mightily in His work! *The Lord wants to speak to His people!*

Once we were waiting upon the Lord, seeking His guidance in our lives and direction as a community, and nothing seemed to be coming through from Jesus! We prayed and prayed and waited! Finally, dad asked Jesus what was the matter and why He would not speak to us. *Immediately*, He spoke, *"I speak to you all the time, but you can't hear me, for your hearts are clogged!"* So we turned to each other and repented of our bad attitudes towards each other and asked each other's forgiveness and forgave each other! As we stood before Him in the purity of our hearts, He began to speak to us and continued for over half an hour! I am convinced, as I read God's Word and as I see the hand of God in the Church today, that we need to hear the voice of the Lord—on a regular basis! This is needed in our daily private lives as well as in the church. We need to be open for Him to speak and to minister through His Holy Spirit. We have been deaf too long! The Church has suffered because God has appeared to be silent. Why? Because hearts were clogged and His people in the Church could not hear His voice any more! But now, as the Lord is clearly pouring out His Spirit, He is speaking, and once more the people of God in many churches are hearing His voice. Many people are getting plugged into the "hot line from Heaven," and the Word of God is beginning to affect them! That Word is teaching and ministering to people. People are growing in faith—and belief.

We dealt with a young man just recently who was starting in a new ministry, an evangelistic singing ministry. The Lord had been teaching him. We had counseled with him over a year before, sharing with him what Jesus was teaching us about ministry. He had been a gung-ho, pentecostal, pulpit-pounding kind of an evangelist who had been involved in show business before he found the Lord. In nightclubs and wedding receptions, his wife and he had performed well, and he still had that kind of style about him—flashy and showy. Yet, he came with his family and ministered at our campground, and we were all blessed! It was still evident that the Lord had something more to do in his heart. God was changing his family from the world's way of performing to His way of ministering! God was also changing their attitudes towards people, their work, and—most interesting—toward their church.

He had been a Catholic at one time and had left the Catholic Church in order to become a pentecostal, and now the Lord was telling him that he had a ministry to Catholics and Lutherans. His wife had been a Lutheran and had left it, too, for the same reasons. What happens when you are an ex-Catholic and walk away from the church and have a negative attitude towards the church? Well, the Lord changes such hearts, and that's what He did to him. He shared with us that the Lord was evidently calling him to go and join the Catholic Church again and to minister there in the power of the Spirit. He went to the Catholic Charismatic Conference and was "blown away." He had never seen Catholics so tuned in to the Lord and so free in the Spirit in his whole life! He said, "Lord, there it is! I'm going to go and do the same thing!" We saw that the Lord had clearly been teaching him! The Lord had been speaking to him, and he had written it all down. The Lord had said, "This is what I want you to do. This is an area in your life I want to change. You are going to get in order this way."

That man had been totally transformed from a man who was a do-it-yourself person who was antagonistic against a particular segment of the Body of Christ. The Lord had taken the antagonism out of his life. He had gone and asked forgiveness for that. He had gone to a priest and asked if he could join his church. The priest told him all he had to do was get his marriage blessed, go to confession, and partake of Communion. But he had said to the priest, "I don't know about that confession bit, but I do want the Catholic Church to forgive me for my rebellious and bitter attitude towards it."

The priest said, "You've just made your confession! Welcome to the church!" It was beautiful!

The Lord is doing strange and wonderful things. He's touching the Catholic Church. He's touching the Protestant churches. He's touching the Orthodox churches. He's touching everybody who is willing to open their hearts—to "unclog" their hearts!

Well, the hearts of this singing family are "unclogged," and because of this, God is speaking to them and opening up a remarkable new ministry for them that is no longer theirs but fully the Lord's. They now are open to the voice of the Lord, and the Lord is molding them into the image of Jesus! We believe that this family is on the way now into an international ministry that is going to bring many, many people into the Kingdom of God! The world is going to be shaken by what the Lord is going to do through them. He is now giving them new songs, anointing their singing. He's been teaching them a new vocabulary to be able to minister to Catholics! He has been showing them that the old "calling of people forward to be saved" is one way for Jesus—but Jesus is not limited to that one way, and He doesn't have to always do it the "pentecostal" or "evangelical" way. He was being shown that the Lord will call His people to salvation any way He chooses, for He knows how to touch people's hearts and create a new relationship with them.

We are blessed to hear that Catholics are being encouraged to accept Jesus Christ as their Lord and Savior and to expect a new and personal relationship with Jesus to be born! We hear of a bishop pointing to the need for evangelistic thrusts to the members of the parishes. This is a miracle. Truly, the Lord is doing a new thing in our day.

15
The Gifts of Healing and Miracles

These two gifts of the Spirit are two more evidences of Jesus at work healing His people as we pray! We were in a conference up in Beaver Bay, Minnesota, in an Assemblies of God church. It was the first Assembly of God we had ever ministered in. We had a blessed time there! The Lord was really good! There was an anointed organist, a lady cop, who was just "out of sight"! She could play that organ like it was a harp from Heaven! We worshiped the Lord in the Spirit that night in such a sweet way—it seemed like angels were singing along with us!

After the meeting, there was a time of ministry, and the people were scattered around the congregation in little groups praying for people in need. I was wandering around and found a lady there who was in need of healing from epilepsy. So we prayed for her, laid our hands on her, and prayed that Jesus would heal her. While we were praying, all of a sudden I felt this bolt of electricity coming through the arm of the woman standing next to me! It just went—voom!—right into the lady under our hands! That was the first time I had ever felt something like that. I said, "Wow, Lord, that was neat! What are you doing?" He had given that lady the gift of healing, a one-time gift for the moment perhaps, to minister to the need of that epileptic lady. The woman was gloriously healed and is well today!

Now, God did not give the gift of healing to me. He did not give it to another lady nearby. He gave it specifically to that lady next to me, "for the common good . . . just as He [the Holy Spirit] wills" (1 Cor. 12:7, 11). God can heal in any way!

As we counsel and come to the close of a session, we pray for healing often, and we anoint the person with oil, lay our hands on him, and say, "Jesus, please heal his spirit. Heal his memories! Heal his body! Lord, set him free!" And God performs a miracle! Every time we pray for someone's spirit to be healed, a miracle has to occur. You can't put their spirit out there on the table and say, "Well, Lord, heal it, please!" The spirit of a man is an intangible object, yet it's a vital reality. It fills man's whole being. God needs to heal that part of man so he can be free.

How about your memories? How does God heal memories? Memory, too, is an intangible thing. It involves data that has been stored in our memory banks somewhere, and only the Lord can get to that! You can't put medication into a man and get to his memories that way. You can't affect the memory physiologically for any long period of time. Only Jesus can touch our memories—by His Spirit! He will heal our memories as we open ourselves to the gifts of the Spirit. Then Jesus goes on from there to heal all kinds of afflictions.

Miracles happen—every time people believe! One of

the blessings of counseling is leading people to Jesus! Many people come who have never really made a commitment to Jesus Christ as their Lord and Savior. We have the privilege and opportunity of saying, "Here He is! Jesus is here to minister to you. We are Christian counselors, and we counsel with Christian believers. Would you like to be a Christian so you may receive all that Jesus has for you?"

One sweet, little teen-age girl came last year. A sister in the Lord and I were ministering to her, and we discovered the counselee had come point-blank out of the world. Her brother had come a couple of weeks previously, and the Lord had given him a "Jesus overhaul," and he was an entirely new man. His sister kept saying, "What in the world happened to Tom?" Tom had shared with her and said, "You had better go over there to Okontoe and see what's going on." She was working in a restaurant and was on dope and going to wild parties—just living in the world, and enjoying it for the most part! We said, "Lord, how in the world do you want to touch this girl?" We then asked her, "Why are you here?"

"Well, it appears the Lord did something to my brother, and I'd like to know more about it," she replied. We told her we'd be glad to share with her.

Then the Lord began to give us passages from the Scriptures. He began to give us words of knowledge which were passages that would minister to her needs! It was like feeding cake to a baby! There it was, the penetrating power of God's truth. We said, "Lord, this is too easy!" Then she would hear another truth and

receive it without question! She just swallowed it all—
hook, line, and sinker. I said, "You just don't know
what the Lord has planned for you. All the glory in
Heaven and all eternity." Her mind was overwhelmed.
Her eyes were bugging out in amazement! The Lord
was saving her soul—right before our eyes! He was in
the process of changing her life. It was so simple and yet
almost unbelievable. She did not come to us with any
faith. She came with questions and doubts. But by His
Spirit, Jesus was wooing her and drawing her into the
Kingdom. It was a miracle!

She was getting so excited about the Lord and so
joyful we said, "Would you like to receive Jesus?"

She was laughing and said, "Yes, I really would! I
don't know why, but I really would like to have Jesus as
a part of my life!" The Lord had already touched her
before she had received Him. She asked Him into her
heart and prayed and was saved.

We advised, "You need to come back a couple of
weeks from now and get set free from some things.
Today is not the right time. Just be blessed by the Lord
and let Him fill you with His Spirit." She did get blessed
and filled. She did come back and was set free of many
things. She is a different person today. And practically
every person in her family has come for ministry.

These are miracles. Just as spectacular as people
being raised from the dead. People *are* being raised
from the dead—spiritually, emotionally, and physically,
and the Lord is doing the work himself! What is a
miracle today? We believe a miracle is a supernatural
act of God in the finite world in which He transforms

the natural situation and makes it supernatural! That's a miracle, and miracles happen every day as people decide to believe! Praise the Lord!

16

The Gift of Faith

We have already written a bit about the gift of faith in the section where I shared what happened in an earlier deliverance experience. It comes as a necessary tool of ministry. The most graphic illustration I can remember, however, is something I read by Charles Price in his book *The Real Faith* (Logos, 1972). This book describes the gift of faith in a powerful way. Dr. Price had a dynamic healing ministry fifty or sixty years ago, and he was an evangelist as well. God would give him the gifts of faith and healing as he would minister to people who were hurting or wounded—physically, emotionally, and spiritually. Each time he could feel it come to him when he had to pray. He would go down a long healing line, and the Lord would give him this gift, and then he would feel it withdraw after he was finished using it. He felt a touch every time there was a need to minister.

He gave a reason for this phenomenon. If he possessed the gift of faith as a skill or the gift of healing as something he could always call on, he would have gone down the healing lines and healed everybody who was there! (The Lord would have healed through him, he says.) He would not have known whether there was something else involved that needed the gift of discernment. Because that wasn't the case, and it was an individual gift from God for a particular person in need, as he went along, the anointing would lift, and he would say, "Lord, what's going on here?"

In one situation, a little girl was asking for ministry (her mother had brought her for healing), and he wanted to pray for her, but the anointing was gone! He asked the mother, "Do you go to church?"

She replied, "Yes, I go to church."

"Do you know the Lord?"

"Yes, I know the Lord!" He couldn't figure what was wrong, and he was trying to probe and find out why God had lifted the anointing before he could pray for the little girl. He was being led by the Spirit to seek in the mother's life for something blocking his prayers! A lady standing next to her in line received a word of knowledge and said, "Do you go to seances?"

The mother replied, "Oh, yes, I go every Tuesday evening!" There it was. The gifts of the Spirit being used in order to set that whole family truly free. Charles Price adds, "If the gifts of faith and healing had been upon me, without any checkpoint, I would have gone right past the mother, the girl would have been healed, and the mother would never have known it was a sin to go to a séance!" But God set the whole family free!

Charles Price also described a most remarkable healing that was dependent on the gift of faith. A woman was carried in on a board, all bound up with arthritis and another crippling disease. She was skinny as a bone and could not move. She was not able to sit up. There were meetings all week, and the first night she was brought in for healing. As Charles walked over to her, the Lord clearly said, "*No!*" God would not give him the gift of faith to believe for her total healing. "*She needs to receive my gift of faith in order to receive this healing,*" continued the Lord.

So Charles Price said to the lady, "Sister, the Lord wants to heal you, but He wants you to come into His presence and receive His faith so you can be healed. God won't allow me to pray with you right now, because He wants to teach you!"

Every day that woman was brought to those meetings, and a change began to take place in her. She had been in the presence of the Lord, and He was changing her heart and was giving her faith! Charles Price described her experience as being like going into the Holy of Holies. She was walking up the steps, then going into the Temple, and finally going on into the Holy of Holies. He said that on the last day of the crusade, which was Sunday, he had not been planning to have any ministry for healing. But as usual the lady was carried in, and then at that moment Jesus spoke to him and told him she was ready for healing! They brought her forward, and Dr. Price told the people he was going to do something he had not planned.

As he walked over to that woman, he was filled with the faith of God, and he reached out and touched her. She was miraculously healed that very instant! She actually jumped off the board, stood up, and leaped and danced and began praising God. That night literally hundreds of people came forward to receive

Jesus as their Lord and Savior. The miracle was a sign to enable the people to believe. Years later Charles Price got a letter from her. He had often wanted to know what actually happened to her at that service. He wanted to hear how she explained the healing and what she understood about how it actually happened. She wrote, "As you were walking up to pray for me, I had a vision of Jesus. He was walking down a road, and He was almost beyond the range of vision, almost at the horizon. As you reached out to touch me, Jesus turned around and looked at me! As He looked at me, waves of faith just welled up over me, like bathing in faith. It was like an ocean pouring over me as I was being filled with the faith of Jesus; I was healed completely!"

What is the faith of God? After Jesus had cursed the fig tree, He said, "Have faith in God. Truly, I say to you, whoever says to this mountain, 'Be taken up and cast into the sea,' and does not doubt in his heart, but believes that what he says will come to pass, it will be done for him. Therefore I tell you, whatever you ask in prayer, believe that you have received it, and it will be yours" (Mark 11:22-23, RSV). Have faith in God! We were told one day that the real meaning of this statement is "Have the faith of God"—not just faith in God, not man's faith in God, but actually God's faith! "Have the faith of God!" What then is the gift of faith? It is the faith of God!

I once was looking at this passage and said to God, "How in the world could I say to this mountain, 'be thou removed,' and it will go into the sea? I don't have that kind of faith!" I began to realize that in the

102

beginning, God spoke by faith and things were created! The faith of God put that mountain there in the first place, so why couldn't a little piece of His faith move that mountain over? That's the only way it could ever be moved! That's the only way the fig tree could have been cursed, by the faith of God which brought it into life in the first place. We need that kind of faith to minister, so we can see the mountains removed from people's lives.

The Lord began to bring to us people who had been deep in the pit. One day in a prophecy, He told us, *"You're fighting the battle on the front lines. I want you to know you are going to get wounded, but when you get wounded come to me, and I will heal you. I tell you, you cannot be destroyed any more!"* We are invincible people, because we are God's people! "No one can destroy you!" That's the same thing Jesus said to His disciples, "I have given you authority . . . over all the power of the enemy, and nothing shall injure you!" (Luke 10:19). Jesus continued to speak to us, *"When you're rid of all your pride, that which keeps you from being my body, then the gates of hell will fall down before you, and you will walk right in and pull out the captives held there by the devil."* We did not know how to handle such words. We did not want to be walking around in hell! But the next day, the Lord started bringing to us people who were right out of hell! Alcoholics, lost ones from the streets, destitute people who were bound up in sins of prostitution, rebellion, lust, hatred, greed, and pornography. You name it— everything, and some things we had never heard of before! And the Lord said, *"Here they are! Minister to them."*

We needed God's faith to minister to these people, and we needed the power of the Holy Spirit. God had worked in our hearts to prepare us. We knew He was faithful to minister to them when they came. We are still receiving them. These are the ones most people give up on, but they are coming and saying, "Help me please!" and the Lord is doing His work in their lives. He does it! We do not have any power of our own—or faith of our own—to do it. He, the Lord, does it! We need His faith in order to minister to such people.

We encourage you to have the faith of God! Let it come into your life! Ask for it! Every day ask for the faith of God, and let it move in your life!

17

Tongues and Interpretation of Tongues

Tongues and interpretation of tongues are familiar to many people, and yet they are totally strange to many others. As we worship the Lord in the Spirit, and the Lord speaks to His people assembled in His Body, He uses the gifts of tongues and interpretation. In the counseling ministry these come once in a while, as a channel of God's Word to His people. We use the gift of tongues to intercede for the people we are counseling, as we pray in the Spirit together. It's a powerful type of prayer! It is an anointed type of prayer that allows us to do the work God calls us to do. Using the gift of tongues you can often find yourself free in the Holy Spirit, letting Him move through you in this way. It's another way of coming into the courts of the Lord and into the presence of the Almighty to receive His truth.

Tongues have been under such attack by people who are still functioning with the mind only, not spiritually discerning. It is an area of experience that perhaps few have moved in, and yet as we ourselves counsel people daily, we have found that using tongues is vitally important. Let us explain.

We referred to "praying in the Spirit" when we were drawing some conclusions about counseling in chapter five. This is an area of prayer that is too often neglected. We believe this neglect is related to being locked into what we also were locked into before we were awakened spiritually by Jesus' baptism in the Spirit. That same old struggle to "understand" spiritually, and not just mentally, stops many people from receiving the blessings we have as we "pray in the Spirit" right in the middle of our counseling sessions.

Paul was very careful about these matters, yet very strong in teaching the Corinthians the purpose of tongues. We have found full agreement with Paul's teaching in our own experience. (Emphasis added in the following verses.) "One who speaks in a tongue does not speak to men, *but to God*; for no one understands, but in his spirit he *speaks mysteries*" (1 Cor. 14:2). Speaking in tongues is always God-ward. "One who speaks in a tongue *edifies himself* "(1 Cor. 14:4). It builds up the believer. "Now I wish that you all spoke in tongues" (1 Cor. 14:5). It is for everyone. Then look at verses fourteen and fifteen of this same chapter, "If I pray in a tongue, *my spirit prays,* but my mind is unfruitful. What is the outcome then? *I shall pray with the spirit and I shall pray with the mind also*" (1 Cor. 14:14-15).

Being United Presbyterians, we came fresh into the gifts without learned expectations that others from the pentecostal churches may have. We therefore had no axe to grind. We are not trying to make tongues the proof of the baptism in the Spirit or stretch the proof of the value of tongues within our lives. We have simply been led by the Holy Spirit himself into a wonderful, new understanding of all the gifts and their practical dimensions in meeting people's crying needs! Tongues and their interpretation are vital gifts, even though they are greatly misunderstood. We believe this misunderstanding needs to be challenged by those of us who can demonstrate significantly how God taught us to use all the gifts—including tongues—in ministering to His people.

Early in our experience of the baptism in the Spirit, we heard people praying softly in tongues. When we were ministering in a group to persons, we found many quietly praying in tongues, and at first went through all the questions about needing an interpretation. Gradually we began to see and experience the power of God in those meetings, as we quietly prayed in the Spirit and waited on the Lord. A brand-new dimension was added to our lives!

When Jesus began to expand our ministries dramatically, bringing great numbers of people to us, we found it necessary to develop teams of counselors to deal with people more in depth than we could do in public meetings. There was a need for privacy when we were ministering to people's deep needs, which we could not find in our public meetings. Therefore, more time was daily spent with individuals away from the times of "power" in the Body assembled to worship God. We found ourselves needing a closer tie to Jesus. We discovered prayer before sessions was not adequate to meet the demands of the counseling times. We were dealing with principalities and powers, with rulers of darkness, and challenging them by the power of Jesus. We needed a continuous link with God's power that just was not there as we struggled to set people free.

It was in those early days, when so much that was strange and new was almost overwhelming us, and where we found we needed more and more of Jesus even to talk with people about overcoming their trage- dies, that we found ourselves needing to pray in the Spirit. Our prayers in English were said regularly and often, even during the counseling times. But we found we needed something more. As the English ran out, we found ourselves turning to our tongues, our private prayer languages, "praying in the Spirit." We were led to keep our minds active and aware of all that was going on in the counseling, but *at the same time* we were led to "pray in the Spirit." We found our spirits soaring upward in anticipation of what Jesus was saying and wanting to do through us! As we prayed quietly, we found our spiritual awareness of Jesus' power became greatly enhanced. While one team member would be engaged in conversation with the counselee, the other would remain alert and listening with the mind, but fully praying with the spirit. As that continued we found the other gifts of the Spirit began to flow easily. While "praying in the Spirit," we found God speaking to us in words of knowledge and wisdom or prophecy! Now as we continue this practice, our spirits actually begin to lift in such dramatic ways that we find great joy just knowing we are being surrounded by His presence— "plugged in" to His very life! We come away from eight to ten hours of counseling daily, not bushed and men- tally exhausted (like we used to be), but keenly aware that Jesus is there all day doing the counseling as we remain expectant, praying in our tongues.

It was John, in his remarkable book of the Revelation, who wrote of this same experience. *"I was in the Spirit* on the Lord's Day, and I heard behind me a loud voice like the sound of a trumpet"* (Rev. 1:10, emphasis added). That is our experience, too! When we are "in the Spirit" (i.e., praying in our prayer language, or our tongue), we hear God's voice within us clearly speaking to us and reaching out through us to touch the people who are before us. At times such as these, we have visions and we see clear pictures of Jesus. We will deal in greater depth with these visions and revelations in chapters 23 and 25 respectively. We feel, however, it is urgent to let people understand this new dimension God has taught us about the controversial gift of tongues.

These are the gifts of the Spirit. There are nine of them. Seven of them were used in the Old Testament in the same way they are being used today. Jesus is the author of these by His Holy Spirit. They are the channels of His love and power, and as we use them for His glory, His will is accomplished. We have the power of God in order to be God's people. We have been baptized with the Holy Spirit in order to utilize that power to minister to people. "You shall receive power when the Holy Spirit has come upon you; and you shall be My witnesses" (Acts 1:8, RSV). If we deny that we have that power or say, "Well, Lord, how could you use somebody like me?" we are grieving the Lord. For He has placed His Spirit within us to do the work. He is the "workhorse"! He is the power source for the whole universe, and He desires to change people's lives. If we hold Him inside and say, "Lord, I am unworthy to be used this way," He will not use us, and we will be miserable. But if we say, "Lord, I can't do this work—please do it through me," we get blessed! That's the key. Jesus will do it differently in every situation. He may reveal things to the people you're counseling. He may reveal things to the person who is praying with you. He may reveal things to the person in line next to the person you're seeking to touch, like the experience of Charles Price that we mentioned earlier. The Lord will touch in healing His people any way He wants to, if we are yielded and open to His Spirit!

Counseling in the Spirit is counseling with the Holy Spirit and using His gifts. Without Him we would not even dare to start counseling, for we would not have any power to do the work God intends to do through us!

PART III

Inner Healing

Rev. Denis Audet

18
Inner Healing Begins With Forgiveness

All inner healing begins with forgiveness. The first authority Jesus gives to His disciples is the authority to forgive. "When he had said this, he breathed on them, and said to them, 'Receive the Holy Spirit' " (John 20:22). Now I really believe this was the time the disciples experienced being born again. Later on in Acts they received the baptism of the Holy Spirit (Acts 2). You will notice here they had received the Holy Spirit, and what followed was, "If you forgive the sins of any, their sins have been forgiven them; if you retain the sins of any, they have been retained" (John 20:23). Now that's really authority!

Most of the people who come to us are Christians, and if they are not, they soon become Christians, for Jesus enjoys dealing with His own people. He does heal non-Christian people, working from the outside in. But generally He works from the inside out. There are many Christians who are missing the boat in this area. They do not realize what authority they have. Sometimes they are like the person who was bitten by a rabid dog. The doctor examined her, and it was too late to treat her, so he said, "You had better prepare to meet your Maker." Right away, the patient started making lists of people. The doctor asked her, "Are you making your will?"

She replied, "Will, nothing! I'm just making a list of the people I'm going to bite!" A lot of people are bitter, revengeful, unforgiving—even among God's people. We need to recognize the dimensions of forgiveness. Many times we look at forgiveness, and we do not understand what it's all about. We are like the blind men who were asked to examine a huge elephant and tell what it was they were touching. One grasped the tail and said, "It's a rope!" Another felt the huge feet and legs of the elephant and said, "No, it has to be a tree." Another got hold of the trunk and declared, "Obviously it's a snake." In the area of forgiveness, many of us are like those blind men. We really do not understand the full dimensions of our authority to forgive.

In his book *Love Story,* Eric Segal writes, "Love means never having to say you're sorry." In a way this is pure baloney, but in another sense he is right. If we are not Christians, we do not have the authority to forgive, and forgiveness has no power. But God has given those who believe the authority to forgive. We need to recognize that. This is a God-given authority, a supernatural one. This is where all inner healing—all physical healing, all deliverance—begins. Sometimes God won't speak to us in certain situations. He won't let us use the gifts of the Spirit. He will sometimes say, "Before I speak to you, I want you to get reconciled." Some of the hardest statements Jesus ever spoke concerned forgiveness.

Matthew 18 teaches many important principles

about forgiveness. Peter asks Jesus, "Lord, how often shall my brother sin against me and I forgive him? Up to seven times?" (Matt. 18:21). Peter thought he was being very gracious. In the Talmud some of the Jewish writers spelled this out, "If you forgive three times, that is sufficient." But Jesus' response was, "I do not say to you, up to seven times, but up to seventy times seven" (Matt. 18:22). That is exactly 490 times. What was Jesus really saying? Was it, "Every time someone does you wrong, you're supposed to mark it up and say, 'that's one,' and keep doing that until the offenses total 490?" Of course not. What He was saying is that forgiveness goes beyond mathematics. We need to live in the forgiveness of our sins. Jesus goes on to tell a very strange parable about a king who wanted to settle his accounts with all the people who owed money to him. There was one slave who owed him ten million dollars in silver. The slave could not repay it, so he was about to be sold along with his family so the king could recover some of the money. Then the slave begged for mercy, and Jesus reports that the king had compassion on him and his family and forgave the entire debt. This same slave found another slave who owed him just $18.00 (according to the NAS Bible), which was the man's wages for 100 days! He grabbed that man by the throat and said, "Pay me what you owe!" This other slave asked for mercy, too. But the slave who had been forgiven did not have mercy on the second slave. Instead, he had him thrown into debtors' prison.

Jesus continues the parable with the words that some other slaves heard of these doings and reported all that had happened to the king. The king was furious and summoned the first slave. He said, "You wicked slave, I forgave you all that debt because you entreated me. Should you not also have had mercy on your fellow slave, even as I have had mercy on you?" Then Jesus continued, "And his lord, moved with anger, handed him over to the torturers until he should repay all that was owed him" (Matt. 18:32-34). Jesus appends and concludes this parable with the statement that is a very hard statement, "So shall My heavenly Father also do to you, if each of you does not forgive his brother from your heart" (Matt. 18:35).

Jesus reiterates this teaching in Matt. 6:14, "If you forgive men for their transgressions, your heavenly Father will also forgive you." I once asked, "Lord, you are usually compassionate and you're loving. How can you be so hard?"

He answered, *"You know, releasing forgiveness and receiving forgiveness are all one piece."* He showed me a picture of a water hose. There was a spigot at one end. The Lord said, *"The Holy Spirit is that living water, and as you release forgiveness for other people, you are also receiving forgiveness for yourselves."* That's what Jesus was talking about. Practically every Sunday we all say, "Forgive us our trespasses—or, debts or sins—as we forgive those who trespass against us." It's interesting. You see, as we receive forgiveness unto salvation, we are called to forgive people who have hurt us. That's what Jesus did when He was on the cross. He said, "Father forgive them; for they do not know what they are doing." That's what Stephen did when he was being stoned to death. So are we called to forgive—to release forgiveness to those people who have hurt us.

We find there are many Christians who are hurting, simply because they have never exercised their authority as believers to forgive. It's important for us to see this. But why are believers to forgive? It's important for us to see this also. Why are they hurting? Notice some of the things that happen to us when we don't forgive or when we refuse to forgive, "And his lord, moved with anger, handed him over to the torturers until he should repay all that was owed him" (Matt. 18:34). What kind of torture do we go through when we don't release forgiveness to other people? The Lord showed me what kinds of torture we will get when we fail to forgive. In Eph. 4:30 it says, "Do not grieve the Holy Spirit of God [that's what you do when you do not forgive], by whom you were sealed for the day of redemption." You see, you have received that forgiveness unto salvation, and you are grieving the Holy Spirit when you refuse to give forgiveness. But let's look at the torture many Christians endure, as well as non-Christians. "Let all bitterness and wrath and anger [resentment] and clamor and slander be put away from you" (Eph. 4:31).

Have you ever noticed in a body of believers when someone is hurting, how the individual will sometimes refuse to release forgiveness toward another individual? All of a sudden, he will get a group of people in on it. Then it becomes a matter of gossip and it gets worse and worse. The offended person hurts so much that he wants support from other members of the body instead of caring enough to confront the person who hurt him.

So, holding it inside, he wants other people to join his side and take up the offense. The hurt becomes magnified beyond reason.

"Let all. . .clamor and slander be put away from you, along with all malice [that desire to get even], And be kind to one another, tender-hearted, forgiving each other, just as God in Christ also has forgiven you" (Eph. 4:31-32). It's all one piece. As you release forgiveness, you let the living waters flow right through you—the waters of forgiveness. But if you refuse to release forgiveness, you cut off your own waters of forgiveness. Then you continue to hurt emotionally.

19
Forgiveness
Protects Us Like a Shield

Many people you counsel with are hurting emotionally and are harboring bitterness, because they refuse to exercise their authority as a believer to forgive people. The Bible says, "Bless those who curse you, pray for those who mistreat you" (Luke 6:28). Right away you have a shield. You are no longer affected by that hurt—simply through the act of forgiveness.

Many people have problems with depression. They don't realize this can be the result of bitterness, resentment, and self-pity. Many people are seeking help for depression, when, really, all they may have to do to find freedom is to release forgiveness.

There is something else that happens when we do not forgive. We are not only being hurt emotionally, but we are also being spiritually attacked. You know, if you go back to Matt. 18:18, you will read, "Truly I say to you, whatever you bind on earth shall have been bound in heaven; and whatever you loose on earth shall have been loosed in heaven." That is a great deal of authority. Many people look at this statement only in terms of deliverance, but really that passage is set in the context of forgiveness and reconciliation. Do you know you can bind people—by your unforgiveness?

You see, when you forgive people, you are engaging in spiritual warfare.

I can recall one situation when a young woman who had experienced rejection came to us. There was a "cord of rejection" binding her. Her mother had experienced rejection, and her grandmother had experienced rejection, too. After we explained what forgiveness could do, she said, "I choose to forgive my mother for the way she treated me. I release forgiveness to her." Later, she phoned us, and we discovered that in a matter of weeks, she, by the act of releasing forgiveness, had seen God reconcile three generations. Her grandmother became convicted, all of a sudden. She phoned her daughter, recognizing the need for them to be reconciled, because they had not communicated for several years. She said, "Would you forgive me for the way I have treated you?"

Her daughter was quick to respond, "Yes, I do." Then the daughter came under the same conviction and called *her* daughter, who had started it all by her releasing of forgiveness, and said, "You know, I've treated you badly, and I really didn't show you the love you needed. Would you forgive me for the way I treated you?" Here were three generations experiencing reconciliation—simply because one woman was counseled to exercise her authority as a believer to forgive. Recently, she told me she was able to get reconciled with her sister, too. You see how that works? It's sort of a chain reaction.

We need to recognize that forgiveness is also the beginning of deliverance. Paul says, "Don't let the sun go down on your anger, and do not give the devil an opportunity" (Eph. 4:26-27). At another time he wrote, "Whom you forgive anything, I forgive also . . . in order that no advantage be taken of us by Satan; for we are not ignorant of his schemes" (2 Cor. 2:10-11). You know, Satan's schemes are such that he would like to tie us up in knots. He would like us to live our whole lives on a scale. On one side of that scale would be guilt (or blame). On the other side would be our hurts.

We have couples who come to us hurting deeply, and we can almost tell how much they're hurting by the way they sit on our couch. If they are really hurting, they sit as far apart as they can—that is, until they get the "Jesus overhaul." Each blames the other for the hurts. "You should have seen what he did to me." Or, "If you had to live with a woman like this you'd understand how much she has hurt me."

There it is—the scale Satan wants us to live by. Hurt—blame! Hurt—blame! We can listen for hours to the reasons why people are hurting. But the real reason they hurt is not because of what the other person did so much as it is their own refusal to forgive the one who hurt them. Does this speak to you? Satan's scheme is for you to live your whole life in a war of hurt—blame. God does not want you to live on such a scale. He wants to eliminate it. He just wants you to say, "I forgive," and that supernaturally and automatically eliminates that Satanic scale. You don't need to justify yourself, because when you attempt to justify your hurts you still hurt. God says, "Just forgive!" "Bless them that curse you, and pray for them which despitefully use you"

(Luke 6:28, KJV), and, when you do this you experience His protection. This is what happens to many people. They not only hurt emotionally, but their whole lives are bound up by Satan. And they cause other people to be bound up, by their refusal to simply release forgiveness.

A woman came to us who was deeply hurt. Not long before, she had understood and accepted the reality of Jesus and had been baptized in the Holy Spirit. She was a young Christian. She described her husband in the best way she could, and even though she described him in this manner, he seemed to be really unpleasant. She said, "You'll never get my husband to agree to meeting like this."

We replied, "Let's start with seeing if you are willing to release forgiveness for your husband. Are you willing to try?"

"Yes."

We counseled her and encouraged her to believe God was working through her forgiveness. A week later her husband came for ministry. He did not receive everything at that time, but seeds were planted.

Another woman came and received ministry. Later, the Lord prompted me to write a letter to her explaining how she could engage in spiritual warfare. All the members of her family had released forgiveness to the father, who had really abandoned the family. I had encouraged her to pray for a supernatural attitude of submissiveness, pointing her to 1 Peter 3, where wives are encouraged to be submissive—even to husbands who are not believing. So that husbands might be "won without a word by the behavior of their wives" (1 Pet. 3:1). I had encouraged her to let her light shine, so her husband could see her good works and then glorify God. So, in a very real sense, she was letting God in on a vital action that needed to happen in that family. Because she was one flesh with her husband, she could get together with her prayer group and bind the spiritual forces that were binding her husband. Her letter in response reported that her husband was coming back home for Easter! This is simply spiritual warfare—but it had been launched by her choosing to forgive her husband. There is power in forgiveness!

In releasing forgiveness, we are really preventing Satan's darts from striking us and actually protecting ourselves emotionally from any bitterness, resentment, and self-pity (which are Satan's baby sitters in the first place). In releasing forgiveness, we are not binding people by our unforgiveness. Remember, "If you retain the sins of any, they have been retained" (John 20:23). It is also a part of ministry to deliver people and to open them up for God's love. Loosing or releasing salvation upon a person will, many times, open that person to receive the reality of Christ in his life. Many women come to us who have been praying for years for their husbands or children, with no evident results. When they choose to forgive their husbands or their children for what they did to them, their husbands or children often become open for salvation.

20
Physical Healing and
Ministry Blocked

What else happens when we forgive—or choose not to forgive? Many people come to us asking for healing—physical healing. We need to realize that physical healing can be blocked simply because of unforgiveness. Bill Jr. and I, plus our wives, held a marriage seminar in Cedar Rapids, Iowa, and a woman who was bent over in an arthritic condition was present. She had received all kinds of counseling, both secular and semi-Christian, and nothing had helped. She had all the psychological answers (more than we could ever drum up or even think of). But the bitterness in her life was still very evident as we talked to her. As she chose to forgive her husband, and many of the people who had hurt her, in this act of forgiveness (and she was clearly aware of what was happening to her physically), she began straightening up. She was no longer bent over!

David understood this, too. In Psalms 32 he says basically the same thing. "How blessed is he whose transgression is forgiven, whose sin is covered! How blessed is the man to whom the Lord does not impute iniquity, and in whose spirit there is no deceit! When I kept silent about my sin, my body wasted away through my groaning all day long. For day and night Thy hand was heavy upon me; My vitality was drained away as with the fever-heat of summer" (Ps. 32:1-4). You see, David was being affected physically.

Doctors tell us that most of our diseases start with the attitudes we have. "Psychosomatic" is a word that is frequently used. Many forms of sickness are the result of our attitudes. David goes on to describe how all this changed and how he got relief from his sickness: "I acknowledged my sin to Thee [he might have said, "But when I *finally* acknowledged my sin"], And my iniquity I did not hide; I said, 'I will confess my transgressions to the Lord'; And Thou didst forgive the guilt of my sin. Therefore, let everyone who is godly pray to Thee in a time when Thou mayest be found; surely in a flood of great waters they shall not reach him. Thou art my hiding place; Thou dost preserve me from trouble; Thou dost surround me with songs of deliverance" (Ps. 32:5-7).

We are not only affected emotionally, spiritually, and physically—but the way we are used by God is deeply affected. There are many people who want to minister in the power of God. There are many who want to exercise the gifts of the Spirit—and yet one basic thing blocks them from being used by God—their failure to be reconciled with people. There was a man in one of our meetings who was all fired up for the Lord, was baptized in the Spirit, and said he wanted to go out in a dynamic evangelistic ministry to the world. But the Lord spoke to him that night and said, *"My son, I want you to begin with your wife and ten children!"*

Jesus says, "If two of you agree on earth about anything they may ask, it shall be done for them by my Father who is in heaven" (Matt. 18:19). The word "agree" in Greek means "whoever is in symphony." Whoever is in harmony on earth about anything that they shall ask, it shall be done for them by the Father. It is not just a question of whether a certain person should be healed. In the agreeing, you should be in harmony with each other—reconciled, forgiven.

At a Full Gospel Business Men's Fellowship International meeting where I spoke, a woman came up after the message and said, "I'd like to be used as a proxy for healing for a good friend of mine."

I said, "Surely, I'll pray with you." As I started to pray, I suddenly felt as though I had cotton in my mouth. I just could not get the words out. I started again and still I could not pray. Then I said, "Lord, what is the matter?"

The Lord spoke to me, *"Ask her how she is getting along with her husband."*

"How are you getting along with your husband?"

She looked at me and became really angry. She asked, "What does that have to do with it?" She was a big enough woman that if she had wanted to she could have hauled off and hit me really badly. I responded, "Well, before we go any further, I needed to ask you that. The Lord seems to be prompting me to ask you."

She then started to melt a little bit and said, "Well, my husband and I aren't getting along too well." Then she poured out her heart—and her husband, standing nearby, poured out his heart. Then they forgave each other, and after they were reconciled, the woman announced that they were celebrating their thirty-fourth wedding anniversary that night. I rejoiced with them and said, "Isn't this a nice way of celebrating? God will now use you as proxy."

As we started praying, the words just flowed. It was so easy to pray then. But God had not been able to use that woman until she was in harmony with her husband. She had agreed about the healing of their friend, but they themselves were not in harmony. We believe there will never be any renewal in the body of Christ or in homes unless there is harmony, as we live together in the forgiveness of our sins.

These are some of the things that can block our ministry when we are not reconciled with one another. There are so many people who want to minister in the power of God, but their lives are a shambles. God will sometimes let them have a little taste of the joy of the ministry, but more often than not He will say, *"Get right with your own family. Get right with your friends. Get reconciled; then I'll use you."*

I would like to finish our thoughts on forgiveness with a testimony of what happened to another lady several years ago. I remember being called to her home and finding her weeping. I sat down with her at the kitchen table as she was drinking a cup of coffee. The first thing she said to me was, "I no longer have any love for my husband."

My first reaction was to say, "Well, surely you must have some love for him." But as I was thinking about that statement, the Holy Spirit said to agree with her. "I agree with you—you don't have any more love for your husband." She went on to say that that very afternoon her husband, out of spite, had done an incredible thing. It was sort of the capstone of their whole life together. She had lots of flowers all around the yard which she really loved dearly. Out of spite, that afternoon her husband had taken his lawnmower and mowed down all her flowers. He had destroyed their love just that same way.

She said, "You know, we haven't been husband and wife physically for a year and a half."

All of a sudden I felt the Holy Spirit leading me, causing me to say, "I really agree with you. Emotionally, your husband has destroyed your love. But do you believe that Jesus could still love your husband?"

She thought about that for a while and said, "I'm not sure."

I continued, "Let me tell you, the Bible says, 'God demonstrates His own love toward us, in that while we were yet sinners, Christ died for us.' (Rom. 5:8). Now even though your husband has destroyed your love, Jesus still loves him." Then I asked her a question, "Is Jesus in you?"

"Yes, Jesus is in me. I am a born-again Christian."

Then I said, "This same Jesus loves your husband, and He is in you. This same Jesus tells you to love your enemies. Do you suppose you can love your husband through Jesus and forgive him?"

She thought quite a long time about that and finally said, "I guess so." Then she began praying a very simple little prayer which I'll never forget. She said, "Jesus, you know I no longer have any love for my husband,

and yet I know you have that supernatural love—that love that believes all things, hopes all things. That love that never ends. I know you are in me, Lord; and because you are in me, I choose to forgive my husband—just as you have forgiven me. Lord, I just ask you to plant in me a seed of your love for my husband."

In less than a week, she had called to report, "Praise the Lord! God has given me a new love for my husband. And what's more—he's my lover!"

That's the power of God! That's the power we have as Christians. That's the power we need to help other people learn to exercise, so they are not tied up emotionally. This power prevents people from being victimized by Satan and living their lives on a scale of hurt—blame. It helps them not to blame others and bind them up with their unforgiveness. It is a power that enables us to be healed and to experience the blessings of a forgiven life.

21

Healing of Memories and Wounded Spirits

Forgiveness opens up the areas of our lives that need healing. Our souls (our minds or personalities, our consciences, or our wills) need to be healed, too. The Bible has a lot to say about this area. "For as he [a man or a woman] thinketh in his heart, so is he" (Prov. 23:7, KJV). Many times our thoughts can overrule the things of our spirits. We have already mentioned that frequently our minds and hearts become clogged. God wants to speak to us, but because we have dwelt on our problems instead of dwelling on Him, we remain "clogged." Forgiveness opens the door to dealing with problems that are stuffed in our minds. You see, God wants to be Lord over the whole person. That includes the body, soul, and spirit. First Thessalonians 5:23 might be paraphrased this way, "We are to render our spirit, our soul, and our body blameless before the coming of the Lord." In 2 Cor. 10:5 this is stated another way, "We are taking every thought captive to the obedience of Christ." Often, we pray that we may submit our minds to Jesus.

Many times our minds are overwhelmed by problems. Have you ever seen people primping as they see their reflections in a shop window? They are not really looking at the displays in the store window, but with enough background light they are attending to their own reflections. In the spiritual realm and in the mind, many people are not able to get beyond their own minds, because of their backgrounds and the problems in their lives. Many people can't hear the voice of God. But Jesus made the promise, "My sheep hear My voice" (John 10:27). Many people wonder, "Why can't I hear the voice of God?" They are hurting, and there are things in their minds that block His voice. Our minds are like computers. Much of the good and much of the bad that we have experienced—including some of the hurts—have remained in our minds, in our memory banks. Now Jesus, through the Holy Spirit, wants to heal our memories, too. That is part of the walk in Christ. He wants to transform our minds. "Do not be conformed to this world, but be transformed by the renewing of your mind, that you may prove what the will of God is, that which is good and acceptable and perfect"(Rom. 12:2). Our minds need to be transformed, and part of this transformation involves exercising our authority and asking Jesus to heal our minds as well as our spirits. This we call healing of memories and healing of wounded spirits.

Many times (we have touched on this in chapter one) an individual may try to do the healing of minds through mental gymnastics. It just does not work, because that's part of the problem. Jesus said, "He that loseth his life for my sake shall find it." (Matt. 10:39, KJV). Now what is the meaning of "life"? It comes from the Greek *psuchē,* from which we get our word "psyche" or mind. Minds need to be transparent to things of the Spirit, because "God is spirit, and those who worship Him must worship Him in spirit and truth" (John 4:24). We must be ruled by the Spirit, not by our minds or our interpretations of how we think God would rule. We limit God by our minds. Many of us feed too long at the Tree of Knowledge instead of feeding at the Tree of Life—which is Jesus.

God wants to transform our minds so our minds can become transparent to the things of the Spirit. We need to recognize that the mind cannot heal itself. There is such a thing as soul power, and we recognize that. Satan, many times, will use our minds. In many occult practices there will be temporary healings. You must pay the price inevitably, however. Many people use the psyche to get a kind of healing. In voodooism, a lot of the power experienced is "soul power." We need to let our minds be in the service of the Spirit. Too many times, because of the hurt we have repressed in our minds, we are confined to the realm of the mind, rather than the realm of the Spirit. We need to be open to the Spirit.

Paul says, "This I say therefore, and affirm together with the Lord, that you walk no longer just as the Gentiles also walk, in the futility of their mind, being darkened in their understanding, excluded from the life of God, because of the ignorance that is in them, because of the hardness of their heart" (Eph. 4:17). Many times, part of the reason we are not able to function properly is not just because we have not released the Spirit in our lives, but because we are hurting in our minds. The mind needs to be healed by God. Many people, before they get the renewal of their minds, and before they hear the voice of God and are used in prophetic utterances, need to be healed of all the hurts and hang-ups they carry with them.

There was a young man who came to us, and the Lord gave me a word of knowledge about him. I said, "You have been hurt by women, and you hate women."

The man said, "I don't believe that."

"Well," I continued, "I might be wrong, but let's ask Jesus, because He wants to heal your mind." I put my hand on his head and prayed, "Jesus, please bring to memory any hurts in his life that need to be healed." Immediately that young man had a flashback of that hurt and the girl who had hurt him. Then he said, "Yes, you're right." Then God healed him. God wanted to heal his memories, and since that time he's been able to hear the voice of God. God began using him in prophecy. But the open door came when he was healed of his memories. He could not move out in the Holy Spirit until he was healed in his memories by the Holy Spirit.

Many times we minister to people with problems concerning lust and pornography. God will heal them, but often it is a slow process. One time we ministered to a person who had been experiencing all kinds of lustful dreams. Even after receiving the baptism of the Holy Spirit he still had those problems. We just asked Jesus to heal his memories. We also told him that Satan would like to make a last-ditch effort and would probably bring all these dreams and lustful thoughts to his mind again. "You need to know that Satan is being threatened." And sure enough, that's what happened. He went home, had a dream, and had all the lustful things come to him again. But he exercised his authority as a believer over Satan's attacks through dreams, and gradually they all departed. Jesus was in the business of transforming this man's life. That is a real process. It is one of the things we need to realize as we ask Jesus to renew our minds. In this process we need to exercise our gift of praying in tongues—also we need to immerse ourselves in Scripture. We tell many people to start meditating on God's Word. "I will meditate on Thy precepts, And regard Thy ways. I shall delight in Thy statutes; I shall not forget Thy word" (Ps. 119:15). This is one way in which our minds are renewed.

This is one reason why Teen Challenge, for example, has been so effective in helping lost young people find a new life. They teach these troubled individuals to meditate, to study, to memorize the Word of God. And the world is shocked to hear of their phenomenal success in drug rehabilitation, when other institutions of our society are happy to have 5 percent succeed in getting free from drugs, sex, and lives of tragedy.

One man came to us having problems with "flashbacks." He had come to the Lord and had married a beautiful Christian girl. But every time he loved his wife intimately, he would have flashbacks of all the women he had sinned against before becoming a Christian. God showed him that he needed to get into His Word. As he did this daily, the flashbacks were soon gone. They left him completely.

We need to recognize, too, that when we are counseling people in terms of healing of memories, preventive measures must also be used. In essence, Jesus told us to guard our "eye-gates" and "ear-gates." If someone has a problem with lust, he needs to get rid of all the pornography. It is a matter of discipline. I'll never forget one person in the Lord who had received the baptism of the Holy Spirit, and when I asked him to preach in my church a year after he was baptized in the Spirit it sounded like he had swallowed the Bible. Wisdom was coming from him. It was simply leaking out of him. Once, we were driving in a car with some young people, and one of them was talking about certain movies that were X-rated. I made a comment about the need to guard our eye-gates and ear-gates. God wants us to protect our minds from such things; the garbage we pick up remains with us unless we allow Jesus to heal our memories and teach us to stay away from this kind of garbage. The youth said, "I don't think that's going to affect me. I feel adult enough that I can handle these things. That just shows me what God has redeemed me from."

The brother who had had problems in this area did not let that comment go by without an answer. The wisdom of God literally poured from him. What he said at that moment has left a lasting impression on me, because it was clearly a word of wisdom. He said, "You know, I used to feel that way, too; then one day I was reading a book that was kind of questionable. I had gone to a movie that was also questionable, and the Lord spoke to me. He said, *'Joe, would you let your little brother look at this book and also go to that movie?' "* Joe said, "No." Then the Lord asked him, *"Why?"* Joe replied, "He's just a little child. He's innocent." Then the Lord said, *"Joe, you're my son, and I want you to be even more innocent than your little brother."*

We are to be as wise as serpents and as innocent as doves. So, you need to be careful as you counsel with people who are coming out of that kind of background. If they still have an interest in that kind of life, part of the counsel you give must include their need to learn to protect their minds—in what they read, see, and hear. Because the healing they seek from Jesus is not going to "take" unless they let the process of renewing their minds go forward by guarding their minds from evil.

God wants to heal our memories. He wants to heal our minds. He wants our minds to be transparent to the things of the Spirit.

Most of us Christians who come from academic backgrounds have a problem. We too often limit our faith by what our minds can understand about God. Our faith is in the service of our minds instead of our minds being in the service of our faith! That's why simple people who cannot brag about their brain power are often used so powerfully. They do not let their minds get in the way. We don't mean to be anti-intellectual. We are simply stating a fact. Too often our minds get in the way of God using us. God gave us minds, but they are to be renewed. Our minds are not supposed to reflect only ourselves and our problems; we are to see the "Light" beyond ourselves.

What about the spirit—the vital part of our make-up? Scripture says, "The spirit of a man can endure his sickness, But a broken spirit who can bear?" (Prov. 18:14). "A joyful heart is good medicine. But a broken spirit dries up the bones" (Prov. 17:22). "A joyful heart makes a cheerful face, But when the heart is sad, the spirit is broken" (Prov. 15:13). "The Lord is near to the brokenhearted, And saves those who are crushed in spirit" (Ps. 34:18). This is a promise. "Many are the afflictions of the righteous; But the Lord delivers him out of them all" (Ps. 34:19). There are many Christians who need not only healing of their memories, but they also need to be healed of their wounded spirits.

God wants to heal your spirits. We find many Christians who don't believe what Jesus meant when He said, "These things I have spoken to you. . .that your joy may be made full" (John 15:11). They have highs and lows. They go to one conference after another to try to hold on to those high times. There are no lasting effects in such efforts, because of their wounded spirits. D.L. Moody was once asked, "Why do you have to be filled with the Spirit over and over again?" He replied, "Because I leak." We see many leaky Christians. Moody had been viciously attacked and ridiculed for his flamboyant style of ministry and his fracturing of the English language; he was a cobbler by trade with almost no education. Yet, America and England know well the powerful way God used Dwight L. Moody to call His people to belief.

We see people daily who are deeply wounded in their spirits. They often find themselves on the verge of tears. They are up one day and down the next. They struggle to live on an even keel but find that experience a thing to be desired only. We see beautiful people who really love Jesus and have turned their lives over to Him and yet find themselves saddened often and unable to live in the joy of the Lord. These people, Jesus tells us, have wounded spirits. They have been injured by some force that has touched them deeply in their spirits and left them "wounded." That force may just be a loved one who deeply disappointed them. It can be Satan himself, who caught them in a moment of weakness and accused them unmercifully. It can be the experience of being accused falsely by a friend and unable to get free from that lie. It can be some sin committed years ago that has never been dealt with by Jesus and has been left there to fester, leaving them wounded spiritually.

Jesus has taught us how to deal with these. It is a simple matter of anointing them with oil and praying that Jesus will heal their wounded spirits. We stand in awe at how quickly such healings take place. We see people, as we touch them with oil and pray for their healing, begin to melt and cry deeply as their wounds are healed, and joy comes to them so beautifully. It always surprises us. There is a lifting of their spirits in a visible way. People often begin to laugh and cry at the same time. Then a glow of peace enters them, and we see them leaving with broad smiles, with their heads lifted, truly free. Many tell us they have a feeling not only of well-being, but they feel something within their chests move and the pain leaves.

We do exactly the same with people who need healing of memories. We have already, in the counseling time, taken them through their hurts and life experiences, recalling those memories that have kept them in bondage. When we reach the time for ministry, we simply anoint them with oil on their foreheads, making the sign of the cross, then we ask Jesus to move in on their memory banks. We ask Him to pull out all those memories that have caused pain, disappointment, fear, distrust, panic, and hatred (all those that we have already discovered in the counseling time) and to heal their memories. The prayer may go something like this: "Jesus, here is your loved one. You've already revealed the areas of pain in his life, and we ask you now to take this one right back to the time when he was in his mother's womb and move him right through the experiences of birth and early childhood. Please take away all the pain and rejection, the disappointments, the fears. Take away from his memories all that has been used by Satan to hold him and keep him bound. Please heal him, Lord Jesus."

The miracle of healing takes place before our eyes. People feel lifted out of their bondage right then. Many discover that within a few days they can recall all those experiences that caused them pain, but there is no pain left in them. It is remarkable. Subsequent chapters further demonstrate this miraculous ministry of Jesus.

PART IV

How God Implements His Counsel

Mr. Darrell Hiatt
Rev. Bill Barr, Jr.
Rev. Bill Barr, Sr.
Rev. Denis Audet

22
Cords of Iniquity

God gave us a very strong Word as we were praying before presenting the material you are reading at a seminar in Wayzata, Minnesota. He said, *"I have a particular and special anointing for each one of you who speak tonight, because the message I want my people to hear and understand is very important."* Bill, Sr., summarized this message, "This is a special revelation for this time in God's plan—for this very time itself!" There really has never been such a massive Satanic attack upon God's people, because until now God has not been pouring out His Spirit in this way on all people. Therefore, the need for discernment and direct communication with God through His gifts is very great.

Not long ago, my wife made a list of things in my life that needed improvement. Unfaithfulness headed the list.

"Yes, it's true!" I said, when I saw the list. "I'm a mess, and unfaithfulness is something I've struggled with over and over again, but it simply doesn't change!"

Recently, in a meeting, I mentioned my struggle with unfaithfulness, among other things. My wife, Murlene, quickly whispered, "Did you hear that gasp?

They thought you meant you had been unfaithful to *me!*" I promptly corrected the misunderstanding, "No, not that! It's my unfaithfulness to the Lord! In those things that I said I would do and that I would try to change!" I would ask God for help, and I would pray over and over that something would change. But there I was—still bound by something. I know now I was bound by "cords of iniquity," which finally were cut away from my life in the first counseling session at Okontoe Fellowship. Let me tell you how I found freedom!

When I first went to see Bill, Sr., and his son, Bill, Jr., they must have thought, "Well, here comes a psychologist, and he's really going to be bad!" So they brought in a third minister! But it turned out to be beautiful! Absolutely beautiful! My anniversary in spiritual counseling began as a counselee, and, believe me, if you really want to learn this method of counseling, submit to counseling and receive God's blessings out of it!

I went up to Okontoe Fellowship in St. Cloud, and when I returned, Murlene was flabbergasted by the changes she saw in my life! On the way up I had been defeated, depressed, and I could hardly see light! On the way back the car sputtered, and I said something I thought I'd never say to any car, "I rebuke you in the name of Jesus! Get out of there, Satan, and run off into the wastelands of the world!" I had finally discovered where to send him and all his servants! This was the biggest help!

Have you ever cast out some demonic spirit that's been hassling a person and later found that spirit right back there working at it again? You rebuke it and say, "Get out!" and then, the first thing you know, you turn around and say, "Hey, it's back again!" Now I understand that this happened because we did not know where to send them or what to tell them. It's reassuring to find out you can send them into the wastelands of the world, stuck there until the judgment of Christ, and know they can't even come back. As I began to pray this way with people and to speak to them about those spirits, it really blew my mind. I had heard all these things before. I had read all I could about deliverance, but this kind of spiritual counseling is the neatest thing in the world. It brings deliverance and freedom from bondage so quickly that even a psychologist doesn't know it took place! I was so happy when deliverance came to me through the cutting of "cords of iniquity" in my past!

We simply moved right into my problems. After about twenty minutes in that initial counseling session, Bill said, "Gee, this is neat! We've covered more in twenty minutes than we usually do in three or four hours! This is going to be great!" But they kept right on working with me as they do with other people. If they have to stop for lunch, that's all right. They eat lunch with their counselees and then keep right on working. They schedule themselves to spend up to five and six hours with each counselee, if necessary. (Note: In recent years God often shortens the time necessary to help His people find freedom. We are now functioning more easily in all the gifts, and His answers come more quickly!) We prayed and waited and asked the Lord what other things might be the real roots of the problems. The Spirit of God must reveal these roots to us. And He did on that first day for me!

There are many things one can learn through taking counseling courses, and you can get a lot of clever ideas and ways to get at some of these problems, but, believe me, this counseling in the Spirit is the most powerful kind of counseling I've ever seen or experienced in my life! It is a real gift and revelation of God to His people for today!

During that first counseling session, we went back over my background and discovered a number of things I was harboring unknowingly in myself, particularly a "wounded spirit." I would get all fired up, and it seemed like I was all set to go and make a big step forward. Then I would find myself far away from those first experiences I had had with Jesus, and something seemed always to hold me back—to be stuck on me! Those are the "cords of iniquity." They are just like rubber bands tied to you, and they pull you back to "ground zero"! For some reason, I was not learning how to walk in the Spirit and walk on the basis of what I had learned and achieved through the counseling I had received before. When those "cords of iniquity" were cut and I accepted a new order of life, learning to live dependent upon the guidance of the Holy Spirit, I experienced victory.

23
Visions and Prophecy

The things that began to amaze me included what I thought would be the root of the problem (the way I was seeing it in myself), but I learned that my perception of the problem wasn't necessarily the way it really was! This is why it is so important to have the gifts of the Spirit operating and for all to be open and waiting for God. As God began to name the roots of my problems, we began to realize that the "wounded spirit" I had carried all the years from a very early age had been affecting all sorts of relationships and feelings. Yes, even in my walk with the Lord! I would never have dreamed such would have been possible.

As we came to a time of prayer for my "wounded spirit," all of a sudden, Bill, Sr., brought out a boom-type microphone and put it up. I thought, "Now what are they going to do? Wire me up? What are they going to do, shock me? I've seen shock therapy, but I've never seen this before!" Then out came a black box, and I thought, "Good grief, what is that, a shock box?" Then I saw Bill put a tape in it, and I thought, "Oh, thank God, it's just a tape recorder! But what are they going to record?" You know, I've been through counseling before, and that day we had been at it for many hours, and I felt we were pretty well satisfied that we had accomplished what we could. I thought, "These guys are dingbats." I didn't speak all these thoughts, but I'm sure now that if I had, they would simply have said, "Don't worry, we are just going to be ready. For when we start praying for you and we renounce those things and cast them out and anoint you for healing of your 'wounded spirit,' God will speak to us."

As we started to pray—just like that—I saw a picture of a beautiful white table! It was a "vision." Now a vision doesn't have to be something with which you are knocked over as was the case with Peter and his vision on that rooftop. It was something I saw in my heart. It was just suddenly there. I had my eyes closed, and yet I could see in my mind a beautiful white table, and around it were all the disciples and Jesus too. They were having a wonderful meal. They were so happy, but I kept looking down at His place, and I noticed a kind of goblet, a chalice for drinking, made of bronze. But on one side of it there was a great gash! Something had hit it and slashed a hole in it. Right then the Spirit said to me, *"That's your wounded spirit!"*

I asked Him right away, "How can you heal that?" At that very moment, the three ministers were praying for my "wounded spirit" to be healed. Then Jesus, in the vision, just took His hand and placed it on the gash, and I knew it was red-hot under His hand. The metals just melted and fused together into a perfect shape. It was so real to me in my mind right then that I sort of jumped back inside, certain I was going to get burned! I felt certain, as my spirit was being healed, that it was going to hurt me! But this did not happen at all! I saw Jesus touch that cup and then take His hand away and set the cup down so it could be filled and used to bless Him. My "wounded spirit" was hindering the joy of the Lord.

When that thought got to me, it really hurt! I said, "O Lord, you know I never really understood that I was spoiling your happy time. Forgive me, Lord, and I thank you for healing me and that you can now rejoice in Darrell Hiatt! Hallelujah!"

The next week, my wife was prayed for, and she, too, had a terribly "wounded spirit," which went back to the time when her mother became pregnant. Her mother already had two children, and it was the middle of the Depression, and her father wanted her mother to take something to abort those twins she was now carrying. She refused to do so, but right then, at that early age, a hurt or a "wound" had developed in that fetus, a spiritual wound!

God showed me another picture as we prayed for Murlene to be healed. I saw Jesus sitting at the same table again, and before Him was that same bronze goblet. There was a plate, which I remembered the week before had not been there. Jesus had had no plate to eat from in the previous vision. This time there was a plate, but it was broken! It was a beautiful white plate, looking a little like porcelain to me, but it was broken in two! Again I said, "Lord, how are you going to restore it?" He said, *"Just like this."* He took it in His hands and just put the two pieces together, and click, it was perfect! As we shared this vision, after praying for Murlene's wounded spirit, we realized that there we were together—the cup, Murlene, the plate, and me—serving the Lord together, all because our wounded spirits were healed.

Then I understood why the tape recorder was there, for at that moment the prophecy began to come. I have experienced this many times since then. At the moment when the work is finished and the prayers have been spoken, God often speaks in detailed and lengthy prophecies. God spoke a specific word to Murlene, telling her He dearly loved her, because He even knew out of which ovary her egg had come, and where it was implanted in her mother's womb! He knew her before she began! Even before the egg was fertilized.

God wants to make himself known to us. You may be reading this and saying, "Oh no, it couldn't be!" But it is true! God wants to make himself as well-known to us as we are to Him!

A most striking way through which God makes himself known to us is in "visions." That night in Wayzata, as these thoughts were being presented, I had the unique experience of having yet another "vision." I had never seen an angel. I had never seen Jesus standing before me. I do have a dear little daughter, however, who had seen Jesus come into her room and sit on her bed. He told her, a week after we had lost her sister, that her sister was all right, for she was with Him! Then He left her room, and Margaret ran into my room at 6:00 A.M., in the darkness of a Montana winter morning. I knew the minute her feet hit the floor that something serious had happened! It was with firmness and definiteness that she came running into my room, shouting, "Daddy, daddy, Jesus is in my room!" I sat up in my bed and said, "I've got to see Him!" All I could think was, "I'm going to see Him!" I jumped out of bed and ran with all my might into the other room! Uh-oh—I had just missed Him! I wanted to see Him so much—but I had just missed Him!

That night in Wayzata, however, Jesus showed me himself! Right up in the shadow of a huge cross that was suspended over a large altar, He showed me himself! I could see a beautiful technicolored picture of Him! I saw all that in my heart, for I felt Him speaking to me, *"Look, I'm right here blessing everybody, just like I promised you earlier when you prayed. I'm pouring myself out on you."* At once I thought, "That's neat, I wonder if anybody else can see Him!" Then I realized I wasn't seeing a literal picture. But I looked up there, and to me, out of my heart, it was actually a picture of our living Lord!

24

Laying on of Hands—
Agreeing Together

God's Word tells about laying on of hands for many purposes. Jesus frequently touched people—even lepers! He touched eyes, ears, crippled limbs. He even knew when a woman with an issue of blood touched Him in a huge crowd, for He was aware of power going out from Him. He told His disciples to lay hands on the sick, and they would be healed. Through His brother James, He told the elders to gather together and pour on a little oil, laying hands on the sick, and He promised they would be healed. He also said that any sins they had committed would be forgiven (James 5:13-16).

The laying on of hands is not a gimmick! It is a holy act commissioned by Jesus, and we are honored to be able to do it. In itself, humanly speaking, it is a beautiful thing to lay on hands for healing and simply to pray for people. It's the most marvelous expression of our love for people that we can possibly conceive.

A psychologist who came to my office told me he attends a massage group. He got so much out of it. I said to him one day, "I've been enjoying people touching me and showing me love and laying hands on me and praying for me for years in this charismatic renewal. You don't have to go out to some massage parlor where everybody purposely gets together to try and give you a little bit of feeling and love by touching your dear old body. You just come to a good prayer meeting, and you'll get a lot more than that! They'll be touching your spirit and your mind and your heart—your whole man!"

Agreeing together as to what should take place is another way we see God implementing His counsel. In Matthew's Gospel we read, "If two of you agree on earth about anything that they may ask, it shall be done for them by My Father who is in heaven"(Matt. 18:19). We have discovered great power as we have believed this Word from Jesus. Not only do the enemies of man flee, but those who "make harmony (or create symphony)"in their agreeing find a strangely beautiful bond and love for each other. We believe this is a blessing of God. These are some of the beautiful "fringe benefits" that come from obeying God and living in expectation of Jesus doing exactly as He promises to do in the Bible.

One of the things that really blesses my heart in a spiritual approach to counseling is the fact that the counselee is able to take charge of his life as spirits are identified. The counselor may lead the individual in a prayer to teach him how to drive out evil spirits; this helps the counselee take charge by giving him a form to follow so he won't flounder. This not only relates to the counselor and the counselee agreeing together, but to the authority we have as believers in Jesus, the Lord of our lives. Many people need to learn this authority and to learn how to exercise it over evil forces that try to hold us in bondage and destroy God's plan for our lives. To go away from a time of counseling with the awareness that you have such authority and the right to use it is a very remarkable feeling of security.

As a psychologist, I greatly desire to help people learn to cope with life, and when I see this happening through the transfer of authority from counselor to counselee, my spirit rejoices. There need be no desire to cause people to be dependent on the counselor. Rather, great stress must be put on people to cause them to see Jesus dwelling within them through the Holy Spirit. Jesus wants to dwell within them in a dynamic way, just like He prayed to the Father, "I in you and you in me" (John 15:4, 5 paraphrased). Something deeply important happens when people begin to believe this. Fear has to leave. Feelings of inferiority fade away. An awareness of one's great value as a child of God begins to bring a great peace. A great sense of well-being pervades us when we let Jesus be the Lord as well as the Savior of our everyday lives.

Murlene and I went to a Women's Aglow meeting recently, and both of us shared with the audience our views about spiritual counseling. As we were ready to leave after praying and talking with a number of people, one lady came back in. She was Catholic, and I had been talking with her that evening. She had been in the charismatic renewal for about four years, and her husband was just beginning to get into it, too, and he was beginning to know the Lord deeply. Her children were finding Jesus, too. She was a very dear person. As she came up to me, I said, "What can I do for you? I thought you had already left the meeting."

Downcast, she replied, "I got out in the parking lot, and the Lord said to me, *'Go back in there and speak to Darrell.'* "

When I asked her what it was about, she replied, "I really don't know, but when we were trying to identify what spirits were harassing us and learning how to cast them out with that special prayer, I couldn't think of a thing!"

We had prayed earlier for this meeting, and one of the leaders had specifically prayed, "Lord, get rid of the spirit of confusion in the people's minds here." I remembered that prayer and realized it was for that beautiful Catholic lady who had returned in obedience to God's voice! A spirit of confusion was binding her. She could not identify anything that was harassing her through all that meeting. As I prayed with her, I did something I love to hear others do, and anybody who has been around Bill Barr, Sr., at Okontoe frequently learns to do this. The first time I heard him do it in Burnsville, I burst out laughing! I remembered that experience as I prayed with this lady. I said, "Spirit of confusion, get out of here right now, in Jesus' name. Out into the wastelands of the world!" Immediately, everybody around me began to laugh. I asked them what happened, and they said, "We got so blessed when you said that. Let's go home. We got all we need!"

I continued to pray with the lady, and, as I closed my eyes, I had a vision of a woman on a tightrope going across Niagara Falls carrying a balance pole. She would have been doing beautifully, except for the five huge steel balls that were in a fish net on her back. Everytime she attempted to balance herself, that net of big steel balls would swing out and nearly destroy her balance. I could see from behind her and knew she was panic-stricken from the struggle she was having.

I stopped right away and shared this vision with the Catholic woman. She said, "That doesn't mean a thing to me."

I responded, "Well, I've got that vision and I'm going to pray for the woman I see in it, because I believe this is what the Lord is showing us."

Somewhat reluctantly she agreed, "Okay, I'll pray with you." One of the things you learn to do in spiritual counseling is to open your eyes once in a while! I used to think that anytime I was going to pray I had to close my eyes! Needless to say, I've learned differently!

As I began to pray for that woman on the tightrope, I saw a yoke come down and rest upon her shoulders. The steel balls were put in containers on each side of the yoke, evenly distributing the load! The yoke fit that woman perfectly, and I audibly described the vision as it appeared to me. As I prayed, I looked over at the lady. Her face was flushed and she was crying, but she did not make a sound. I thought, "Well, something good is happening. Some healing is taking place that she didn't realize she needed."

I continued to pray for her, and as I did so, in the vision I saw a man on the other side of the falls. It was the lady's husband, and he had his hands opened wide as he reached towards her and waited for her to jump to him. She easily walked the rest of the way on the wire and blithely jumped into his arms. Then together they walked into a beautiful brightness on the other side of that great trial.

I said to the woman who came for prayer, "Well, that's it! You're all the way through! Isn't that neat? Praise the Lord!" Then she cried out loud! I asked her what the Lord had shown her, and she eagerly answered, "I didn't realize it! I have been torn between this renewal and my own church where my dedication should be." Instead of letting the flow go between the two as she should have, she had gotten into a place of bondage over the dilemma. It was all or nothing, one way or the other, and she was aching and hurting inside over the struggle. In her heart she had never realized this. That night, Jesus revealed it to her.

25
Special Revelations

I had an experience that opened up to us all the awesome reality of how God is determined to communicate His truth to us. As we look back on what happened, we believe God revealed to us an eternal truth. The biblical evidence to support this truth is getting stronger daily. But it seems, at first glance, to be in conflict with the traditional ways God works.

One evening, I was speaking to a congregation, and out of my mouth came the words, *"There is no love in judgment."* I was shocked by this statement, for I knew it was a word of God, but I could not understand it. I simply stopped speaking and said, "I don't know whether I can defend that word." I then asked the people if they would study this statement and pray that God would give us wisdom about it. At first, you may say, "Well, how can this possibly be true? Doesn't God judge all our actions? He is a God of judgment and wrath. He is the one who will ultimately judge us in the final day—Jesus himself will. We know these Bible truths. How do all these fit in with what God now speaks, 'There is no love in judgment'?" Does this mean God is going to judge us without love? God help us if that's what He will do! As I began to think about these ideas and wondered what God was trying to say, I became convinced that He had revealed an essential and eternal truth.

Herbert Mjorud, in his book *Authority to Believe,* had this identical truth revealed to him in a similar way. He was praying before preaching one day, " 'I ask you, Lord, for the power of the Holy Spirit. I believe now I have that power. Thank you, Lord Jesus, for anointing me with the Holy Spirit. Amen.' There was the inner-heart conviction that I was the Lord's servant and His power was now within me. I had been. . . an apologist for the Faith because of my legal training. I had preached as a defender of the Faith. Now the Lord inwardly impressed upon me, 'You do not have to defend me or the Faith. I have called you to proclaim the Faith.' From that point I saw man in a new light. *I saw them through the eyes of love and not judgment.* Suddenly I was excited and eager to communicate this Gospel of Love. I walked out to the sanctuary and looked at the people sitting there. I sensed a new compassion for them. When I preached the sermon that morning, there was a 'calm' sense of urgency. There was a new liberty."

Let me show you how this same "revelation" came to us. Maybe this will help you become aware of what we are discussing. We were dealing with a young lady, and, as we looked at her, we were aware that Jesus had already touched her life significantly. She was a very beautiful young lady, and we wondered what her reasons were for seeking counseling. I told her, "It is very evident that the Holy Spirit is working in your life."

She quickly replied, "Oh, yes! I gave my life to Jesus just three months ago, and ever since, He has been changing me." The radiance of Jesus was shining from her face in a most beautiful way. When I asked her what she wanted, it was a great surprise to hear her say, "I want to get clean."

As she told her story, we were flabbergasted to hear how tragic life had been for her. She had been married at eighteen, divorced at twenty-one, and, until three months previously, she had been living with a succession of men for two years. It was hard to believe what she was saying. Then the old patterns of our past began to rise up in our thoughts. Judgment entered in for a moment, and we began thinking about why such a beautiful person would be so stupid as to live that way. But just at that moment, Jesus flashed a "huge color slide" before my mind. It showed Jesus ministering to the woman taken in adultery. She was cringing in fear as she waited for the stones to be thrown by her accusers. But just to Jesus' right, all the stones lay where they had been dropped by those who thought they had trapped Jesus. To my mind of judgment Jesus should have been saying, "You filthy woman, get out of here! I've saved you from death. Now, go before they return. Go, sin no more." But that isn't what Jesus said. Tenderly, He asked, "My daughter, where are your accusers?" And she said, "There are none here, Lord." Then Jesus so tenderly said, "Neither do I accuse you! Go and sin no more."

All through that evening, for two hours or more, every time I found thoughts of judgment rising in my mind, that huge "slide" would reappear. One time I saw Jesus looking over His shoulder at me, and He clearly said, *"I was set up for this one! The Pharisees dragged her right out of a bed where she was committing adultery. She is guilty as charged. She deserves to be stoned to death, according to the law of Moses."* Then Jesus lovingly turned and said, *"My daughter, where are your accusers? . . . Neither do I accuse you! Go and sin no more!"*

I spent the entire evening, right in the middle of counseling that beautiful young lady, watching a slide show! It was always the same picture; always the same clarity of understanding what Jesus was saying; always the same gentleness; always acceptance of that prostitute as His "daughter." He kept saying, *"Where are your accusers? Neither do I accuse you. Go and sin no more."*

That "revelation" began to crowd in upon us, and we tried to explain what our experience had been to many people. I was speaking about this and trying to show people there was no judgment in my mind, and yet it didn't make sense to me, and then He spoke those words out of my own mouth, *"There is no love in judgment."* I said, "Teach me, Lord." That's when I began to get into this study of what God was saying to us.

As I was seriously pondering these matters and asking Jesus to show me more, He spoke these words to me, *"The typical man today lives daily in a world of judgment. He begins his day by facing a bathroom which has already been messed up by several sons or daughters. By the time he gets to the breakfast table, he has made many judgments about his children. He is upset as he sits down for breakfast where his wife, trying desperately to please him, spills the eggs. He, in anger and judgment, shouts at her, 'Forget breakfast! I'll catch a bite to eat on the way to the office!' He is so upset and full of judgment, by the time he starts driving his car, he begins to push too fast, and the next thing he knows, a policeman is flashing his lights at him and telling him to pull over for a speeding ticket! He finally gets to work late, and as he tries to pull himself together for the day's work, he is called in to see his supervisor, who proceeds to warn him that this being-late business had better stop—or he might be faced with his job being abolished."*

That illustration reveals the nature of judgment, and it is the world most people appear to be living in. There is little, if any, love in it. That is why we believe what Jesus said through Paul, "Do not be conformed to this world, but be transformed by the renewing of your mind!" (Rom. 12:2). The world we see around us is one of judgment in all its ways. And we are called to live in this world—but not to be "of it." A large part of learning how *not* to be of the world of judgment is to let Jesus renew our minds, giving us His mind and His attitudes towards life. He teaches us to *respond* to the situations and people around us with His love and understanding, not to *react* against what comes in the form of judgment upon us. He is teaching us to stop defending ourselves, to look upon our accusers—those judging us—not with more judgment (which is "reaction") but with the mind of Jesus, which only responds with love. This is the way He shows us what His Kingdom is all about. As the "finger of God" casts out the forces that constantly judge us, the Kingdom of God comes upon us. We find ourselves living in a new world that is more beautiful than we had ever seen before. The way of living that specializes in judgments and put-downs and struggles with people who are always taking advantage of us is to be "transformed" by the God who loves us. We then are to find ourselves living peaceful, happy lives—controlled by love only. Could this happen elsewhere than in Paradise? We believe it can happen, and is happening, today when the "Kingdom of God comes upon us"!

An earlier experience formed a preface to this revelation. A couple who had already made up their minds to get a divorce came to us as the "place of last resort." They were sitting on our long couch and were as far apart as they could get from each other. As I sat across from them and heard the judgments they were throwing at each other, I felt I was watching a Ping-Pong match. Back and forth.

"He doesn't know how to fulfill me any more."

"She doesn't know how hard I've tried. Why, I've bought her everything she ever asked for."

Back and forth with their accusations. In the middle of their disagreement I heard Jesus ask me, *"What's going on here?"*

I replied, "What do you mean, Lord?"

Again He spoke, *"What are they speaking to each other?"*

I thought awhile, getting back into the Ping-Pong match, looking back and forth, and finally I said to Jesus, "Judgment. There isn't any love being expressed— it's all judgment."

And Jesus pointed out, *"Right! Remember this!"* There it was, the same truth, but not so dynamic as the word He had revealed out of my own mouth later when He said, *"There is no love in judgment."*

I continued to study this with others who were willing to risk setting aside old, prejudiced (pre-judged) ways of thinking about God's judgment. God had me teach this subject over and over again. Each time I spoke, He would reveal more of its deep meanings. One of those times, as I stressed how much of a struggle believing this was for me, Jesus spoke to me in a new way. Kenneth Hagin's book *I Believe in Visions* tells about how Jesus would appear beside him, while he was speaking, and would engage him in conversation. I often wondered how the audiences handled that phenomenon. I pictured consternation in the minds of the people as Kenneth stood up there talking to Jesus, whom they could not see. Now it was happening to me, a longtime Presbyterian minister. It was "instant conversation," which, in some mysterious way, didn't even interfere with the words I was speaking. I heard clearly what Jesus was saying and engaged in conversation with Him easily, while I was still teaching several hundred people.

Jesus said to me, *"I've answered your prayers."*

"What prayers, Lord?"

"The prayer you pray nearly every day with your counselees."

"What do you mean?"

"I have answered your prayer, 'Lord Jesus, I submit my mind to the Spirit of God within me. I ask you to renew my mind according to your promise in Rom. 12:2 and grant me the mind of Jesus Christ.'" As I was receiving all this, tears gathered in my eyes, and I could not go on speaking for a few moments. I must have stopped, for I remember saying to Jesus, "Do you really mean you have granted me your mind?" I found myself overwhelmed by the meaning of this announcement and couldn't hold back my emotions very well.

Then Jesus spoke, *"Now, don't get excited over this. This is just the normal Christian life."*

That is often the way He deals with me—ever so gently, but firmly, too, in the clear way He reveals His truth. I began to think about what it means "to have the mind of Christ." I realized it means we are going to think the thoughts of Jesus, instead of always giving interpretations of what we think God means by His Word. We wait on God, and He tells us specifically what He means. If we, then, have the mind of Christ and the gift of faith (which is Jesus' faith given to us by the Holy Spirit), then suddenly *we are a part of God's attitude towards His world.*

I think this is the key to receiving God's revelations of truth. When we submit our minds to the Holy Spirit and expect to have our prayers about being granted the mind of Christ answered, then we begin to look at people with an entirely different attitude. I asked Jesus,

"But, how do you handle sin? How do you deal with Satan's control of people? How do you deal with man and sin? How do you separate men from their sins?"

Then He said to me, *"Of course I judge sin. I judge Satan who creates it all—but I never judge my own creation. I only love it!"*

Now that's hard to grasp. I asked, "How do you separate it all? If you have a clobbered-up person, controlled by Satan, how do you separate man from the real evil that is in him?"

He said, *"Read Hebrews 4."* Now, if you read Hebrews 4, you find this statement, "The Word of God is living and active and sharper than any two-edged sword, piercing as far as the division of soul and spirit, of both joints and marrow, and able to judge the thoughts and intentions of the heart. And there is no creature hidden from His sight, but all things are open and laid bare to the eyes of Him with whom we have to do" (Heb. 4:12-13).

As I recalled those verses, Jesus spoke again to me, *"If I can separate soul from spirit, there certainly is no problem in separating sin from sinners."* See this? This is an eternal truth. But how do we, human beings, still caught up in the flesh, receive all the gifts of God? This puts us in an entirely different realm than that which most of us grew up with. We don't "learn" how to separate sin from sinner, to love rather than to judge. *This is a gift of God to those who will believe!* It is in great contrast to how most of us grew up. We learned "how to be good." We were taught to go to church and Sunday school regularly, to read our Bibles and pray every day, not to say bad words but to speak the truth; then we were told if we did all these things, we would be blessed. Isn't that what we all grew up with? How does it fit what God is saying to us today? We must let this truth come upon us. It is not by our power or through our intelligence or by our willingness! It is by the power of the Holy Spirit coming upon us and making us over into the image of Jesus. That puts all of the initiative on the other side, doesn't it?

That may be satisfactory to the idealists, but to the teacher in school who hears a student who did not study say, "God's got to get me through this exam," there is a vital conflict. James tells us that faith without works is dead! What too many of us have bought as the Christian life, however, is that by our good works we can gain faith. That is the doctrine of *karma* that came out of Hinduism and was swept into the Church of which we are all a part. It became a controlling attitude that ruled our churches for centuries. Don't think the Reformation cleared all this up.

This attitude still affects us in all churches to this very day. This doctrine of *karma* is the same doctrine of good works that is very attractive to people. Men *do* get pleasure out of doing good works. Do you hear that? There is blessing in doing good things. This is a very appealing doctrine, but it is in great conflict with what God is now revealing to us. What we are learning is that *it isn't the work we do to earn the grace and blessing of God that matters; rather, it is the work God does in us that prepares us to be a part of His work in the world.* It seems completely turned around, but it has not left out man's part of the work.

Now how does all of this apply to our lives as we relate to each other? Love and judgment are, in essence, mutually opposed. Paul speaks to us about not judging the non-Christian. Jesus said we're not to judge people at all. Judgment implies rejection, a harsh attitude toward people.

When I studied philosophy in school, judgments were critically important. We made judgments about ideas and things, trying to determine which were right and which were wrong. Where did Adam and Eve get into their trouble? Wasn't it because they wanted to know how to decide right from wrong? These are deep matters that God is trying to help us understand, so we can realize how profoundly they influence our attitudes toward each other. Until we allow this divine understanding to come into our lives, we are going to continue to fool ourselves about getting along together in marriage, about understanding our children, about being able to live under the authority of the world and still survive under it. This truth of God affects every relationship we have and everything we do. This is why I consider that simple statement, *"There is no love in judgment"* to be such a profound truth. I encourage you to try to grasp this in a deep way. For what I actually began to understand was that Jesus did not get upset with His people. He did not come in anger against His people, even when they were doing evil things. He always comes with salvation. He comes with love. He always comes to touch us with understanding. He always wants us to respond (not react) to people's needs with the love of God, which changes their lives.

If you are still struggling with your marriage, put this truth into practice, and ask Jesus to make you into a person who is alive to this revealed truth of God. That's why the "walk in the Spirit" is the essential, normal Christian life. It is not natural—it is very unnatural. It is actually supernatural. That's why we have to keep going back to John 1:12: "As many as received Him, to them He gave the right to become children of God, even to those who believe in His name." I think being children of God means we walk in the Spirit, supernaturally able to receive His revelations to make our lives meaningful and fulfilled. The question is this: Will we allow our natures to be changed? That's why Paul talks so much about becoming "new creatures." As we become new creatures, we suddenly start functioning not only in the natural but in the supernatural realm. Then all of this that we are studying begins to make sense. But none of it will make sense until we allow our natures to be changed.

As we look at the deep walk in the Spirit, we find it is not just a neat way of speaking in tongues and occasionally getting one of the gifts of the Spirit. It is not saying, "Look, I've arrived, and isn't it too bad you haven't arrived." What is the essence of that very statement? Judgment! This is where much criticism has come upon Christians from the beginning. It wasn't always that they judged people (although God knows that has happened, too), but other people felt judged by them because they looked like they knew more than they did about what was going on in life. Well, if we seriously walk in the Spirit, the revelations of Jesus should begin helping us discern God's truth. Then His revelations—such as, "There is no love in judgment"—will no longer appear impossible or foolish but will become vitally creative in our lives.

26
Why People Need Healing

In Gen. 2:23 we find a description of Adam and Eve before the Fall.

Then the man said, "This at last is bone of my bone and flesh of my flesh; she shall be called Woman, because she was taken out of Man." Therefore a man leaves his father and mother and cleaves to his wife, and they become one flesh. And the man and his wife were both naked, and were not ashamed. (RSV)

They were at peace. They were created perfect in the eyes of God. They were whole people. They had not sinned. They had the choice not to sin. They had the opportunity to maintain the wholeness God had given to them.

Satan began tempting the woman.

So when the woman saw that the tree was good for food, and that it was a delight to the eyes, and that the tree was to be desired to make one wise, she took of its fruit and ate; and she also gave some to her husband, and he ate. Then the eyes of both were opened, and they knew they were naked; and they sewed fig leaves together and made themselves aprons.

And they heard the sound of the Lord God walking in the garden in the cool of the day, and the man and his wife hid themselves from the presence of the Lord God among the trees in the garden. But the Lord God called to the man, and said to him, "Where are you?" And he said, "I heard the sound of thee in the garden, and I was afraid, because I was naked; and I hid myself." He said, "Who told you that you were naked? Have you eaten of the tree of which I command-ed you not to eat?" The man said, "The woman whom thou gavest to be with me, she gave me fruit of the tree, and I ate." Then the Lord God said to the woman, "What is this that you have done?" The woman said, "The serpent beguiled me, and I ate." The Lord God [cursed] . . . the serpent. (Gen. 3:6-14)

And we might add that man died in his spirit.

We have discussed in chapter three that when a two-dimensional man, which all of us became when Adam and Eve fell, finds the Lord Jesus Christ as Savior and Lord of his life, a spiritual new birth takes place. As we receive the baptism of the Holy Spirit, that new life pours out into our whole being and transforms us. But what happened in Genesis, chapters two and three, is that the relationship between man and God was broken by sin. We, as men and women today, are suffering with the same problem. We are born as sinful creatures into a world full of sin. We have to make a choice to have life and let Jesus renew us and make us whole. When we become Christians, Jesus, in essence, says, *"I have paid the price. You are a new creation of mine."* And then a new life begins! But all the accumulated sin of man still forms a residue in our lives—in our flesh and spiri-tually in the bondage of demonic forces upon us. We, therefore, need a process of cleansing—of being made whole—in order to be the children of God, the warriors of Jesus Christ, people who are victorious over the powers of the devil.

For far too long, we have seen defeated Christians everywhere we go. Many people think everything happened at the time Jesus came into their lives. But they have never received the power of the Holy Spirit. They have not been fully cleansed. They have not been delivered. They have not been healed. They are carrying all kinds of garbage from the past. It is as if they are carrying big loads on their backs—hurts, broken relationships with loved ones and friends, bitterness that is deep within them, resentment, hatred, and rejection. Man is basically a fragile creature who can be destroyed by other people! In all likelihood, you have experienced hurt as you were growing up. If God was gracious to you and gave you a home where you received love and joy and acceptance and forgiveness—a home where you were considered a child of God—then you received a blessing. Your life was not full of tragedy as it may have been for another brother or a sister who grew up in a different family and did not receive such blessings. Their lives were programed for destruction. Most people's lives, we believe, are programed for destruction by the devil—until Jesus intervenes!

The process of counseling in the Spirit is the process of ministering to Christian people the healing that Jesus has for them. It is a healing they have not yet received for themselves. The role of the counselor is to be a channel of God's Word and His power—simply letting the process happen. Healing needs to take place in our spirits, in our souls (our feelings and emotions), and in our memories, as well as in our bodies. We need to be delivered if we have received demonic spirits into our lives. We need to be set free from the bondage of past generations. Free from sin, the iniquity that has been passed down from one generation to the next.

Jesus read Isaiah 61 as He started His ministry: "The Spirit of the Lord God is upon me, because the Lord has anointed Me to bring Good Tidings to the afflicted; he has sent Me to bind up the brokenhearted, to proclaim liberty to the captives, and the opening of the prison to those who are bound; To proclaim the year of the Lord's favor, and the day of vengeance of our God; to comfort all who mourn; to grant to those who mourn in Zion—to give them a garland instead of ashes, the oil of gladness instead of mourning, the mantle of praise instead of a faint spirit; that they may be called oaks of righteousness, the planting of the Lord, that he may be glorified" (Isa. 61:1-3, RSV).

Jesus read this in the synagogue after He had come out of the wilderness. He then said, "Today this scripture has been fulfilled in your hearing." He was saying, "I have come to do precisely these things. I have come to release the captives who have been bound by Satan and who are bound to die!" He has given us life—saved us from the pit—and wants to set us completely free!

During this particular time in history, Jesus is renewing His Church. He is purifying His bride. Remember, it says very clearly in God's Word that during this time, Jesus is going to make His bride spotless! He is going to cleanse her and unite her as his body, so He can be wed with her at His coming. When you consider the kind of people we have all been and the kind of bride the Lord deserves and is looking for, a lot of cleansing must yet be accomplished!

One time when we were worshiping together, the Lord spoke to us through a prophecy and said, *"I come to you, my children, my bride. I desire to come and embrace you and to hold you unto myself. But you look at yourselves and you see how filthy you are and you flee from me. You run away! Don't run away! Let me hold you and heal you and make you whole! The bride must be prepared for the wedding feast and the marriage!"*

We are the bride of Jesus Christ. He is raising up His bride at this time in history. We need to rejoice in the fact that Jesus will bring to us people who need to be healed, people who need to be set free. People who are His sheep but have been abused by the world. People who have been stomped on and mutilated mercilessly. For Jesus loves them and wants to see them become whole. He wants them to be able to stand before His throne as purified lambs. That's what is happening today.

27
The Case of the Woman Who Was Programed by Satan to Die

She was about twenty-five—a handicapped person in a wheelchair. Another counselor and I had the privilege of sharing with her. We saw the Lord touch her in a very special way. As we began to share, we asked the Lord to show us what needed to be done. She then began to relate the things that had happened in her life.

She had had a child out of wedlock and had to give that baby up for adoption. She did not know who the father was, because she had been walking in iniquity. She left college and went wandering in the world trying to find some answers. She got into the drug scene, taking LSD and a lot of other drugs. She found nothing, except hell. She had simply gone "bananas," as many people do. She was not able to cope with the world any more. She was given shock treatments to try and bring her out of her deep depression. One day the doctor encouraged her to go home and visit her parents. When she was at home she found her brother's revolver and shot herself three times—twice in her chest and once in her head as she tried to kill herself!

That was the devil trying to destroy a person God wanted in His Kingdom! And he almost succeeded! Today, she is handicapped because of what she did to herself—under clear directions from the devil!

But now she is a child of God! God knew her before the foundations of the world, and He was waiting for her to come to Him. Yet, after her attempted suicide, she was mad at God. She was furious because He had not permitted her to die! Finally, Jesus revealed himself to her and said, *"I love you! If you had died, you would have gone straight to hell. I love you!"* Jesus became real in her life, and suddenly there was hope again. Suddenly she had a purpose for living. She stopped being only a two-dimensional woman, and she became a three-dimensional person who had begun to choose to live. Things were beginning to look up for her, but she was still suffering when she came to us. She had all those hurts buried deep inside. The times when she had sinned. The times when she had been rejected by her mother and father. She claimed her mother and father had never loved her. She had been lonely and alone all of her life. She needed someone to love her. She needed Jesus to love her! She needed her mother and father to love her. She was wounded deeply in her spirit and in her mind and in her body. She was a hopeless cripple— in three different ways!

Then Jesus came as we met with her, and He said clearly, *"I want to heal you in your spirit, in your memories, and in your body!"* As we counseled with her some very important factors came out!

First of all, we found that all her hurts were related to broken relationships in her life. She had sinned against others by being bitter and resentful towards them when they had been mean to her. She had basically ignored her father and mother because they would not show love to her. Her father had been an alcoholic for years who finally sobered up. But even after he had been set free from alcohol, he still did not reach out to his family in love. He could not love them, because he didn't know Jesus.

Next, she discovered she had a lot of people to forgive, and she also needed to ask God to forgive her for hurting a lot of other people. What we have realized in ministering to people is that the key to receiving healing of any kind is forgiveness. We need forgiveness in order to be saved in the first place. We need to forgive others so we can receive God's blessings. For some miraculous reason, when we forgive and say, "Father, I forgive that person for what he did to me, and please forgive me for my feelings towards him, and please forgive him, Jesus, and make him whole," suddenly all heaven breaks loose upon us. The heavenly door opens up, and the power and love flow, and healing begins to happen in us and in the lives of the people who have hurt us.

We must realize that we bind other people when we refuse to forgive them for hurting us. We bind other people—spiritually tying them up tighter than a drum! You know, it's possible to take somebody and just bind them up so tight with your unforgiveness that they don't have a chance in the Kingdom unless you let them go! The tragedy is that if you bind another person up in this way, you also bind yourself up. We wrap the rope of bondage around our own necks while we are wrapping it around the individual we will not loose with forgiveness. So, for our own sakes, we need to forgive others.

Then we can be free, and God can also bless those we have forgiven. You see, Jesus loves us so much that He has died for us and forgiven our sins. We also need to let that forgiveness flow out into the lives of others! Then healing takes place as we forgive!

The person we have described in this "Case of the Woman Who Was Programed by Satan to Die" had a lot of painful memories. Jesus said He wanted her to be whole, so we prayed for her, anointing her with oil, and we asked Jesus to heal her memories. We asked Jesus to take her all the way back to the time when she was in her mother's womb, to the time when she had had her own baby and had to give it away, and then to that traumatic time when she shot herself. Suddenly, she began to be refreshed! After she had forgiven the people who had hurt her, her memories were still tormenting her! Satan was still using them to keep her hurting. But now—as she was prayed for—the Lord began to lift her spirit. He took away another part of her life that Satan had been using to keep her in turmoil. When Jesus touched her memories, He took the pain all away!

She now faces life no longer bound but free—cleansed! She now is able to live, because Jesus not only healed and cleansed her, but He fully lives in her. She is no longer alone. She has successfully escaped Satan's program of death—and accepted Jesus' plan for life!

28

Jesus Is Still at Work
Setting the Captives Free

In chapter 25, we studied God's revealed word dealing with love and judgment. The words, *"There is no love in judgment,"* will take on deeper significance as we are called to join Jesus in setting the captives free from Satan's control over their lives. This work of Jesus, which began when He was a man on earth, occupied one-fourth of His ministry recorded in the Gospels, and it still continues dynamically through His people who believe. Jesus still loves and, with that love, He draws people to himself and snatches them away from the hassles they find themselves living in. When we are "delivering" people by the power of Jesus, we have to have an attitude of love, or we find ourselves in real trouble.

Everyone is able to say, "I can love people who are beautiful." But what about those who are not so beautiful? Those who flaunt their unbelief. Blaspheme God. Turn against all that they know to be true. Make a mockery of everything we know to be true. With such people, we may ourselves stand up and say, "You can't do such things!" The recognition of the horrible character of evil as it takes control of people must not be turned into a judgment against those people. It must instead turn to love. When that happens, we are in a position of great strength, and people are saved from themselves and from Satan's plan for destroying their lives. They are delivered by the power of Jesus' love as it pours through us to the people He never stopped loving.

Do you remember the story of Robert Ingersoll, the creator of the Ingersoll watches that were so well-known for many years? He is noted in the *American Heritage Dictionary of the English Language* as "Robert Green Ingersoll, 1833-1899, American political leader, orator, and agnostic." He, as a militant agnostic, was violently outspoken against God. He would have large public meetings where he would openly blaspheme God and would cry out arrogantly with a challenge to any member of his audiences, saying, "I defy anyone to come up and prove there is a God. If there is a God [and here he would pull out his famous watch], let that God strike me dead in the next minute." In more than one meeting, he was struck down by some believer who walked up and said, "I don't care whether God will strike you down, but I will." Strong men of God would face him saying, "You can't talk that way about my God." Then they would knock him down.

This story has been told over the years to demonstrate that faith needs a little help from strong men. The idea that if God won't vindicate himself, I'll have to vindicate Him, needs a closer look. We are not into such works. We believe that God will act—in His way, in His time. "God will fight for you while you keep silent" (Exod. 14:14). *The Living Bible* says, "The Lord will fight for you, and you won't need to lift a finger." I think Taylor's paraphrase in *The Living Bible* is most clear, and it fits into what God is teaching us right now. "Will you let Me fight My own battles?" God asks of us. It is not our job to deal with the enemies of God. Now you *will* be dealing with the enemies of God, but you had better believe that God is the one who destroys them, or you are in for some real surprises. Satan will level you. We have that authority in Jesus when we allow Him to move through us. In Jesus! And that *does* change the situation.

Put all this into perspective with love and judgment. We can say, "Well, we are judging whether there is a demon in someone or not." No, we are *discerning* with the gift of the Spirit. You must be on this solid ground, for if you are on judgment ground only, you are in serious trouble. You will be deciding out of your own limited opinion and experience, and you will be cleverly looking for a demon under every bush. We have seen a lot of people get off the track in this work. They will look at everyone, wondering if they have a demon. They will look in your eyes suspiciously and say, "Oh, yes, you must have a demon." Satan loves to do this to people—even good Christian people—to make them confused and appear to be fools. This will happen if you work out of *your* experience and skill in judging the presence of evil forces. Such warfare against the enemies of God must be waged with the weapons and wisdom of God himself. And in the center of the warfare, love—His love for His people—must always be the controlling factor as we reach out to snatch others from Satan's hands. This is where the mind of Jesus must function in your own mind, so you don't cast out a loved one and minister to a demon.

I was asked by a friend of ours to read a certain book dealing with exorcism. They had a daughter who was running wild. We had met them one day when they told us about her. They said, "She's sleeping and living with four men in a mobile home. She is on dope and refuses to come home. She is really freaked out."

I said, during that first meeting, "Well, why don't you take your authority as the head of your family and stand against those lies in your daughter's life? Smite those lies right now! I'll agree with you." We did that and the daughter came home the next day on her own. It literally blew that family away to see the power of God channeled through a believer's faith. We've seen this happen in many families. What I'm talking about is the authority to control the forces of evil by the power and the acts of God. Now if you are still wrapped up in making judgments, you can be greatly disappointed.

The book on exorcism deeply impressed me by giving a definitive list of demons—names I had never heard before. I thought, "I believe I'll cut these pages out of the book and put them in my Bible—so when I'm dealing with demons and casting them out, I'll have a ready reference to all the demons I might meet."

Right then the Lord shouted at me, *"Shut that book!"*

I shut it quickly and asked, "What's the matter, Lord?"

He explained, *"I don't want you to read that book*

anymore. If you need to know the name of any demons—just ask me!"

This may seem like a minor point, but it's the affirmation of what we are trying to say right here. It is God who knows exactly what's going on. You don't have to get spooky wondering if you're dealing with the demons correctly. You don't have to make the demons name themselves. We find they lie like their "father of lies." They hide behind each other and try to make fools of us when we challenge them out of our own expertise instead of the discerning power of God. The demons will have to give you their names as you move in Jesus' name against them. But we don't do that any more. God has taken us out of that type of work. He tells us, *"My power is a victorious power—it has already defeated the enemy, and what you are dealing with in the ministry of deliverance is often just a form of camouflage and fake spirits. These spirits will try to make you believe they are terribly dangerous, but when I expose them, you will see them as they really are— puny, unimportant things to life."* This is true of even Satan himself—because Jesus has the victory and Satan is under His heel.

If you think you are going against a victorious power, and that you have to be smart enough to outwit it in your own strength, then you are going to get clobbered, for Satan does have power—but only the power that you allow him to have. He has more power than a human being—but not more than a son of God! When you are born again, Jesus gives you power to become children of God. This is what we are writing

187

about. It deals with the mysterious realm of the "spooky." But the realm of the "spooky" gets very "unspooky" when, with Jesus' wisdom, you understand who is behind this realm and know him as a defeated power.

We remain grateful to the Roman Catholic Church for its standing firm on its basic doctrines about Satan. Lots of us Protestants thought Satan was just a psychosis or neurosis or an upset stomach. We considered all thoughts of Satan and his powers as superstitious nonsense, no longer viable in a world of intellectual superiority. We bought the lie that Satan, after all, is just the weakness of uneducated people. We assumed that Satanic worship and demonic activity continued in the unenlightened backward areas of the world only. The voodoo rites of Africa and the islands of the sea continue only because of lack of enlightenment, we surmised. We certainly considered ourselves too sophisticated to believe such nonsense.

I have news for you if you still fit this picture of "the skeptical sophisticate." Your reasoning is a lie of Satan to keep you in the dark. There are real powers of evil, and they *can* kill people. They *can* control people. They *can* and do rule people. But only if the people are *not* children of God. Or, they can rule children of God when the children of God begin to doubt or begin to walk in ignorance. It is no crime to have been harassed by demons. Welcome to the crowd. This will happen especially when you begin to "walk in the Spirit." You are going to find out what the "spirits" look like and what they do. You will be surprised at how many spirits there actually are.

One's attitude toward deliverance is vitally important. It is so critically important to develop the right attitude as we begin to talk about the ways we deal with people needing "deliverance from evil forces." It is not just an attitude of mind, but rather it is having the mind of Christ. When you have the mind of Christ, you will understand how He deals with demonic powers. You will see that demons came to Jesus, screaming at Him through the voices of two men in the country of the Gadarenes, "What do you want with us, O Son of God? You have no right to torment us yet" (Matt. 8:28-29, TLB). The demons recognized the Son of God, and Jesus often silenced them. In that case, He allowed them to go into a heard of swine, who, then demon-possessed, killed themselves by running into the sea.

We include teachings about "deliverance" and how to deal with Satanic powers as we teach on counseling in the Spirit, not because we are trying to say to you, "Get ready for the battles ahead of you. You are going to have to deal with all this ugly stuff, too." On the contrary, we are trying to say to you, "This is the normal work of Jesus Christ. One-fourth of Jesus' ministry was devoted to that vital work of "setting the captives free." And that does not just refer to spiritual and physical captives only. It clearly refers to setting people free who are experiencing Satan's hell on earth. This is the "deliverance ministry of Jesus." So don't be afraid of it. It is the work of the children of God to defeat the works of Satan. The Bible clearly states this truth, "The Son of God appeared for this purpose, that

He might destroy the works of the devil" (1 John 3:8). Jesus is still at work destroying the works of the devil, and, as children of God, we can expect to be used by Him in delivering the people of God, destroying Satan's power over them.

29

The Battle Is Not Ours, But God's

We have discussed the authority of the believer in terms of releasing forgiveness and healing memories and wounded spirits. We have talked about this real authority we possess. Many of us are not experiencing this authority, yet God has given it to us so we can be His Body, vitally at work in the world today.

I remember many years ago when I first came into the baptism of the Holy Spirit. That was on a Saturday, and on Sunday the Lord gave me a sermon to preach based on Luke 4:18. I preached on this but didn't really understand the full depths of what the Lord was saying. It was Pentecost Sunday when I preached this first sermon after I had been baptized in the Holy Spirit. " 'The Spirit of the Lord is upon Me, Because He anointed me to preach the gospel to the poor. He has sent Me to proclaim release to the captives, And recovery of sight to the blind, To set free those who are downtrodden, To proclaim the favorable year of the Lord' (Luke 4:18-19). Then Jesus closed that book and gave it back to the scribe. 'The eyes of all the synagogue were fixed upon Him, And He began to say to them, Today this Scripture has been fulfilled in your hearing'" (Luke 4:20-21). That was Jesus' ministry. And Jesus, who is the same yesterday, today, and forever (Heb. 13:8), is still in that same ministry today. He has given us that same ministry, that same authority. To release the captives, to forgive just as we have been forgiven. To heal.

Our topic is centered on that passage, "To proclaim release to the captives." Another word for this is deliverance. A lot of us have heard about deliverance. I came from a very liberal theological background and considered such ministries relegated to those with mentalities appropriate to the Middle Ages. I believed in healing because I had experienced healing myself, in most miraculous ways. I had attended a Kathryn Kuhlman meeting with a very critical spirit, and the Lord, in that very meeting, healed me of a curvature of the spine. I saw all this and said, "Oh, my gosh!" My wife had been healed earlier of epilepsy. I knew about healing, that's for sure. I had heard Dr. Alfred Price, the founder of the Order of St. Luke, and I was ready for such a ministry. But this area of deliverance I had put aside. It may be something for other people, but it certainly was not for me.

When I received the baptism of the Holy Spirit, the Lord showed me this was to be a part of my ministry, too. It was something I just didn't want to deal with, because I didn't understand it. It was something I certainly had never been taught in seminary. But I was put in the position of being advisor to Women's Aglow for a local chapter, and one evening the Lord wanted to teach me in His school of the Holy Spirit that there was a deliverance ministry.

A lovely woman brought another woman who appeared to be wild. I wasn't too sure about how to handle her. I hoped she was going to come for healing—for others had come to me for that before. I became increasingly uneasy and even more so when her escort said to me, "This woman needs to be delivered."

I nearly caught myself saying, "Delivered from what?"

And then the Lord, for the first time (and many of us have experienced the same individually), began to say to me, *"Yes, we're not fighting flesh and blood, we're fighting powers and principalities behind them."* There are many things that we think are from the flesh, when Satan is actually behind them. Lo and behold, Satan really started speaking through this woman. At first I felt like the guy who said, "You know, I have some good news and some bad news. The good news is that I've got Satan on the run, and the bad news is that he's running after me." I felt like running. I felt like the Israelites before the giant. For there was a Goliath before me. I said to myself, "Man, I'm not going to handle this." The hair on the back of my head went up, and I was about to take off! I said, "Get someone else!" But then suddenly within me came these words, "Greater is He who is in you than he who is in the world" (1 John 4:4). With that word came the authority—that welling up of the Holy Spirit within me—and I was able to deal with that woman, even when the demons started talking to me. The other pastor, I'm sure, was just as unfamiliar with the whole matter. He was another Presbyterian minister, you know, and here we were both unexpectedly involved in a full-blown deliverance ministry.

Ever since, I've never tried to avoid this ministry, for the Lord has shown us that we do have the authority. The Bible says, "There was a man in the synagogue possessed by the spirit of an unclean demon, and he cried out with a loud voice, 'Ha! What do we have to do with You, Jesus of Nazareth? Have You come to destroy us? I know who You are—the Holy One of God' " (Luke 4:33-34). Now that must have disturbed the liturgy for that morning. It certainly disturbed the "liturgy" for Women's Aglow—whatever was planned was suddenly postponed by this woman needing deliverance. But the Lord showed us that we do have authority over the demonic realms. I was really nervous about people pleading the blood of Jesus. I thought this was kind of a "slaughterhouse" theology, and it was certainly not my "bag." However, I remembered I had read something Maxwell White wrote about "pleading the blood of Jesus," and at that moment, as I was faced with my first deliverance, I found myself saying, "In the name of Jesus, I plead the blood!" I heard it come out of me. The demons were saying "No" to me but not when, in my new-found authority, I pleaded the blood of Jesus. My theology had been renewed. Now I'm as "bloody" as the rest of them. There's power in the blood. The pentecostals knew this all the time.

I don't want to dwell too long on this, but we need to recognize that we are struggling with principalities and powers, and we need to understand that we do have a God-given authority to defeat these powers. After we begin to understand our authority and use it, these spiritual forces no longer put up a fight.

A woman came to us who had stuff "crawling all over her." A demon spoke through her to me saying, "Why are you smiling?"

I said, "We've won, we've won! You have to get out!" It's a beautiful thing. There is that confidence, because "greater is He who is in us than he who is in the world." Someone received a prophecy recently in which God said, *"Satan may seem like a roaring lion, but when you understand my authority you'll discover he is toothless."* When you submit to God, the devil will flee from you. If you are trying all this in your own power, then forget it. You'll get beaten up, like the sons of Sciva (see Acts 19:13-16).

One of the things that amazes us is that as we've recognized God's power as it is demonstrated in ministering to people, we don't need to go into the rigamarole of making the demons name themselves— unless the Lord tells us to. He gives us the word and tells us to have people cooperate in the deliverance. We aren't doing something to them, especially in the area of deliverance. When we do something for people, the demons put up a fight. They see the ones possessed or harassed as being not willing or not too sure of wanting to be free. But when these people confess their desire to be free, and they rebuke the spirits controlling them by saying, "In the name of Jesus, I renounce you! I sentence you, by the authority of Jesus, to the wastelands of the world," then the devil and his spirits don't put up a fight, because the people are cooperating with Jesus.

Sometimes when we minister *to* and *for* people, we find people who are not sure they want to be delivered. The woman I first ministered deliverance to was not quite sure she wanted to get rid of the spirit of lust. She said, "I've seen that demon, and he's beautiful. Jesus, I don't know." Realizing this, we decided we had better start introducing Jesus first. The Bible tells us that once we have cleaned out the evil spirits from a house we had better fill it with Jesus. There are some people who have forgotten this and have ministered for or in behalf of a person who may not have even wanted to receive Jesus; then the state of that person can become seven times worse than before (Luke 11:20-26). So, we fill them up first with Jesus and then let them exercise their authority as believers. That's what is meant by the Scripture, "Work out your salvation with fear and trembling, for it is God who is at work in you, both to will and to work for His good pleasure" (Phil. 2:12). So there should be no stigma associated with it, like there is with some who feel embarrassed to ask for counseling for fear that there's something horribly wrong with them. No, people who are cooperators in their own deliverance from evil are simply exercising their rightful authority as believers in Jesus.

I was impressed by Kenneth Hagin's book *I Believe in Visions*. One part especially fascinated me. In fact, it overwhelmed me and left me awestruck. He had a vision of Jesus—but all of a sudden a demon started jumping and screaming between Jesus and Kenneth.

Kenneth was waiting for Jesus to exorcise that demon. He could not even hear Jesus speaking because of all the noise coming from that demon. He waited and finally got so disgusted that he said to the demon, "In the name of Jesus, I renounce you—get out of here!" And the demon left; then Kenneth could hear Jesus. He asked Jesus, "Why didn't you get rid of that demon?"

Jesus replied, *"I couldn't! Because I have given you, as a believer, that authority."* He has given it to us. There are many Scriptures that support this statement. Luke 10:19 and Matt. 10:1 deal with Jesus giving this authority to the disciples—an authority to cast out demons along with other great powers. Another verse picks up on this, "Whatever you shall bind on earth shall have been bound in heaven" (Matt. 18:18).

Many people have great hang-ups about this. They make deliverance bigger and more spectacular than it really is—something ghoulish. There are such elements in this ministry, but when you recognize and use your authority as a believer, these are no longer significant, and they no longer bring fear into your heart.

One person we ministered to made a confession before she arrived. "God, if there is anything blocking me, I want it out of my life." She had hardly spoken this prayer when things within her started coming up and began groaning inside of her. She did not understand what was happening, and she turned to a friend, "I know I need ministry." Her friends were really afraid. She came to us, and I could see her sitting down, bracing herself, expecting something terrible to happen. I said to her, "You exercise *your* authority! Renounce these things, and they will go away." You know, I almost felt that this disappointed her. She expected a battle, but one wasn't necessary. The deliverance was nothing fancy! Many people expect terrible manifestations, but we need to understand that when we recognize our authority, Satan is automatically a loser. Satan will do everything he can to wear out the saints in long deliverance sessions that drag into the wee hours of the night, if we do not stand on our authority. When we stand on our authority as believers in Jesus, then it becomes a settled matter—something already accomplished by Jesus on the cross. In this way, it is just like salvation. Just like the baptism in the Holy Spirit. We need to appropriate our authority.

Some people ask us, "How does someone become possessed? Are there degrees of possession?" The Lord has shown us that we need not become involved in trying to determine how *much* a person is possessed or specifically *how* the possession came to be. The term "possessed" actually conveys an incorrect image, for the "demonizing" of a person is a matter of degree. God does not care whether your problem is "harassment" or "possession." He wants you to get rid of the demons. People ask, "How can a Christian have a demon?" There are different ways through which people can be demonized. Continual sinning in a given area will have eventual spiritual ramifications. We usually think of this in terms of acts of immorality, but often it simply involves attitude. Earlier, we discussed forgiveness in its spiritual dimension and showed how a lack of forgiveness opens us emotionally to bitterness, resentment, self-pity, and depression. But if we sin and don't choose to forgive people who have hurt us, we can open ourselves to the spirit of bitterness, the spirit of resentment, the spirit of self-pity, the spirit of depression. It works the same with pornography, lust, homosexuality, and other sins of the flesh.

What are some other ways in which a demon can enter us? Investigating or getting involved in the occult is an easy way to open yourself up for the entrance of a demon. Many who have been involved in occult activities find themselves getting under "curses," as well as all types of demonic influences in their thinking and actions. Deuteronomy 28 describes the curses that follow those who worship other gods. Many times we see this phenomenon in families. Down through family lines we can see three clear types of curses—poverty, sickness, and death. We frequently see these in families involved with the occult, even though their involvement may have been back two or three generations. People open themselves up to demonic activity in these ways. Others become demonized by dabbling in Transcendental Meditation, mind sciences, and the mind-expanding drugs. Such people actually surrender their wills to demonic forces. Hypnotism is another means through which people become demonized. This involves surrendering the mind to whatever control may choose to possess it; under hypnotism, your mind is no longer under the control of your own will. The soul—or mind—is the area where Satan can work, in contrast to the spirit of man, where the Holy Spirit dwells and works. This is clearly illustrated in the Bible: "The devil had already put the thought of betraying Jesus into the mind of Judas Iscariot" (John 13:2, Phillips). We need to understand this. Satan would like to tie us in knots, emotionally. But Jesus works through our spirits to bring peace for the entire man. That is why we are to be ruled by our spirits and the Holy Spirit who dwells in our spirits. So many Christians are ruled only by their souls (minds); therefore, their emotions are in control. Satan can take hold of Christians who are ruled by their emotions and even possess them to such an extent that they actually get under his control. In such cases, Jesus is the only one who can rescue them.

Another area that requires deliverance can be in the realm of spiritual inheritances or "cords of iniquity." I would like you to look carefully at this topic. This may be new to some of you, but God says clearly, "You shall not worship them [other gods] or serve them; for I, the Lord your God, am a jealous God, visiting the iniquity of the fathers on the children, on the third and fourth generations of those who hate Me, but showing lovingkindness to thousands, to those who love Me and keep My commandments"(Exod. 20:5). Did you know that there is such a thing as a spiritual inheritance? Many times we see a spiritual inheritance through which the sins or blessings of past generations are transmitted to present generations. It's sort of like an umbilical cord, through which one generation's sins or blessings have access to another generation. It is an area where Satan functions to try to control people. In this realm, God allows Satan to visit the iniquity of the fathers on the children. We see this demonstrated daily in the lives of people we counsel. Rejection is often transmitted down through three or four generations. Alcoholism often follows through families. Lust is a big area that is used by Satan to demonize three and four generations. People today who are victims of the past sins of their forefathers as well as their own sins need a saving knowledge of Jesus and deliverance from the demonic forces which have had access to their families through cords of iniquity.

Some Scriptures you may want to study clearly relate to this subject: Acts 8:23 ("the bondage of iniquity"); Ps. 18:4-5 ("cords of death," "torrents of ungodliness," "cords of Sheol"); Num. 14:18 ("He will by no means clear the guilty; visiting the iniquity of the fathers. . ."); Deut. 5:9 (a quote from Exod. 20:5); and Jer. 32:18 ("[He] repays the iniquity of fathers into the bosom of their children after them"). The Bible is full of support for the spiritual inheritances or cords of iniquity that can be taken out of the hands of Satan. When this happens, people's backgrounds are no longer able to dominate and destroy them. Jesus has been given to save man from such iniquities. He was crushed for our iniquities (Isa. 53:5).

It is a simple matter to break these "cords." The person involved must acknowledge Jesus as Lord and Savior of his life. Then, along with two or more other believers, he can agree that these cords (he should name them) must be broken in Jesus' name.

30
Jesus Provides Everything—
When He Calls Us

I would like to summarize what we have been trying to proclaim throughout this book. Particularly, we want to reemphasize a basic principle we have discovered which gives both the counselor and the counselee great hope!

We believe, beyond a shadow of a doubt, that when Jesus called us to be His disciples, He provided us with every single thing we need to live in absolute peace, totally unharassed and uncontrolled by the devil. With such total provision there is no reason why we should not be moving forward to do His work according to His will!

This is a principle we really believe in. We get very disturbed—not angry, but disturbed and hurt—when we see people who complain that they don't know how to live! They have confessed the same Lord and Savior we have confessed. They believe God raised Him from the dead, as we do, and they have received salvation. Many of them have also been baptized in the Holy Spirit. And yet we hear them complaining. "Oh, I just can't make it! Why can't I get over these things that control me?"

This attitude is due to the fact that we haven't realized

the extent of our authority. We have not really received all that Jesus has promised us. As I read His Word, He has it all put together. It contains everything that is needed to give us total peace, total contentment—at all times and in all ways! My favorite benediction describes this, "May the Prince of Peace himself grant you peace at all times and in all ways!" I believe He does!

That prayer does not say we are not going to have struggles. It does not say we don't have times when we are going to be wondering. But we have the answers for all such times, if we will keep our eyes upon Jesus!

We know that when we use the authority given us we don't have to worry any more. We see many people who have blown Satan's power all out of proportion, compared to what he really is. He will get as big as you let him. But if you are a believer you have control to shrink him down to nothing and to step on him! You have that authority, without any doubt. Most people think we have to be very careful when we are dealing with evil. They say, "Oh, am I ever scared! I know I won't sleep good tonight. I wonder what the demons will do because of what I had to do today." We don't buy that any more! We know Jesus has made our security possible. He has already answered all those questions. He has the full answers, and He offers them to us freely. He gives everything we need to live securely. He said, "I give you *authority . . . over all the power of the enemy, and nothing shall injure you*" (Luke 10:19, emphasis added). You see, He even promises protection for us!

In 1976, Jesus spoke to us in a long prophecy. He

really "did a number" on us that day! He actually talked to us for about an hour and a half! We recorded it all, and we had a beautiful experience. We still go over that prophecy and find deep meanings we missed before. He spoke much about pride. Does Jesus ever work you over about pride? Pride is something we all struggle with. That day He told us what pride is all about. We had never heard it explained that way before. These are Jesus' words to us on July 29, 1976.

"I call you to a new type of discipline! No longer the pride of privacy, the pride of a different way of looking at things, the pride of wondering whether you are accepted, the pride of self-pity, the pride of resentment, the pride of withholding that which was deep in your heart! No longer this, my sons! Put away all pride! Just let me be your life in the days ahead! When you stand with me, without any pride, without any false hopes, without any private concerns that keep you from understanding me and being my body, then I tell you, the gates of hell will fall flat down, and you will walk in and bring out the captives who are there by the devil."

Jesus really said that to us! Then He continued, *"Don't be afraid! Expect to do battle, and don't be surprised if you get wounded. Just come to me, and I will make you whole! For there is nothing that can destroy you any more!"*

Do you believe what Jesus says? That is total provision! That's where God is. All the fear goes out of life! Jesus just removed fear! "If God is for us, who is against us?" (Rom. 8:31). Really, think of this! This began to make more sense to us the more we had to deal with using our authority fearlessly.

Not long ago we had a chance to test this promise of Jesus. Denis Audet had been working in the deliverance of a young lady along with Bill Morel. They worked until about midnight and came out quite weary. The young lady came over to say hello to me before leaving, and as I met her, I discerned another demon and "kicked it out" right away. We had known this girl for some time and had seen many demons exorcised from her. She had been so controlled by demonic forces that she had become an obviously unhealthy person. She was not pretty to look at. She actually looked a bit like a mentally retarded person, and we often felt she just wasn't being real with us. She was depressed and was hard of hearing, too. She had a peculiar look in her face, but when those demons were cast out of her, her facial appearance began to physically change. Have you ever seen that happen? It's a beautiful miracle!

The next day Denis was counseling all day, as we do daily, and towards evening he said, "I feel like my right arm has been pulled out of its socket! I have a headache like I've never had before!" Immediately, the Lord quickened to me that prophecy of 1976. I said, "Jesus, you told us that if we were doing this work, we would get wounded, and we should come to you and you would heal us. We claim that right now for Denis, in Jesus' name!" *Instantly,* it was done! Headache gone. Shoulder completely without pain.

Another aspect of this was interesting, too. The girl who had been delivered called the next day and said, "I've just been to the doctor to see whether I have angina. I have such a pain in my left shoulder and left arm that I thought maybe I was having a heart attack or angina pectoris!"

The Lord spoke to me right there and said, *"Do it!"*

So I said over the phone, "Dear one, you were just pulled out of hell by that arm! Let's rebuke it in the name of Jesus. In the name of Jesus, be gone, pain!" Again, *instantly,* it was gone from her arm and shoulder!

It's all a question of belief. It's a question of whether you have a belief that is without limit, a belief in the Lord who is limitless. If you are content to deal with a faith that is limited to what your mind will allow it to be, you are too limited. Jesus used to say to us, *"I can't tell you everything now, for you won't be able to handle it."* Have you been on this walk with Jesus? Is this how He speaks to you? This is what Jesus is doing. If you will let Him speak to you, He will direct every step of the way, in everything you do. If you take time to *listen* to Him, He will direct you. If you are always talking to Him, you will have trouble hearing Him. This is why we regularly wait on the Lord, praising Him, studying His Word in specific ways, laying before Him the questions of our lives and the decisions of our entire community. And as we wait quietly upon Him with specific needs spelled out before Him, *He comes to us and answers all our questions!*

He said it another way to us one time. *"If you keep looking at me, Satan can't even look in your direction, because he can't look at me!"* That put a new dimension into our living. If we keep our eyes on Jesus and walk along believing He is able to do everything, Satan can't do anything to us. Satan knows his limits. He knows that if we are with Jesus, he can't even look in our direction, for he doesn't dare look at Jesus! He can't face Jesus. Believe that! Use that power! You have that power in Jesus!

I was asked to teach one full day in four sessions, each one was one hour and fifteen minutes in length. This was in a Lutheran church and they were having a workshop day where many pastors and Sunday school teachers and religious education workers were gaining new ideas for the fall programs in their churches. I knew only one person there. I felt like a total stranger, and I was the only one who was dealing in the area of the Spirit. They asked me to speak on "Cults and the Occult."

About the middle of the summer before I was to speak, Old Slewfoot came around to me and said, "Watch out! Your job is to proclaim Jesus Christ, not to put down the devil or expose who he is!" I heard that and decided I'd better present this to my elders. So, we met and had a day of prayer and asked God if I was supposed to teach and expose Satan. I asked, "Jesus, do you want me to go and expose Satan, when you've called me not to expose him, but to proclaim you as the Lord of all?"

He said, *"Yes, you are supposed to go, and as you teach, I'll show you why you are there."* This was confirmed by all the elders, and so I went.

I had to drive a long distance from another conference we were conducting. I left at 7:30 A.M. and got to the workshop just in time. I felt strange, but there were many people who were willing to listen to what I had to say about "Cults and the Occult." Jesus used that time in a beautiful way. I had reproduced an outline of various cults and the occult and I passed copies of it to the audience and began teaching. Before I was finished that day, I had talked five hours! We had the largest group of that day, and people expressed deep interest in what Jesus was sharing through me. But what God revealed to me that day deserves close attention by those of us who are related to the churches of our day! The *only reason* the occult is active today and the cults are proliferating and spreading like wildfire is because *the church of Jesus Christ is not demonstrating the power of God!*

That is the truth of God! We have all the power that is in the universe at our disposal, but we are often not using it. Our children are running away and searching for truth in counterfeit faiths.

I get really excited when I realize people can finally wake up to the fact that we do have all authority in Heaven and earth! For we are connected to Heaven, and we can stand before the forces of evil and say, "Get out of here in the name of Jesus," and they must leave! We can stop people who are blaspheming the name of Jesus! Yes, even in the middle of a sentence they must stop when we exert the authority God gives us. We once stopped a pastor in the middle of a sermon as he was speaking against the Holy Spirit! We prayed silently, "Forgive him, Lord! Stop him! Don't let him commit a sin against your Holy Spirit!" We have seen such men stop right there, confused and unable to go on, wondering what happened. You have that same authority. I adjure you, I plead with you, to learn what your authority is and to use it for the glory of Jesus. We must stop living like nonbelievers!

We really believe we're not like many who are "peddling the word of God" (even though sincerely); we are doing it "as *from* God, we speak *in* Christ *in the sight* of God" (2 Cor. 2:17, emphasis added). Now what I want to get across to you is something that if you receive it into your spirit it will totally change your way of living! You are the Body of Jesus Christ, *if you will receive all of what Jesus offers you!* And if you receive it, *there is no force in Heaven or earth or hell that can stand against you!* Heaven will not stand against you, and hell cannot! You are backed by all the forces of Heaven when you stand in the belief that you are not just "peddling the word of God," but rather speaking it "in Christ in the sight of God"!

31
The Vital Mission of the Church in Our Day

I am convinced that counseling, as we have been discussing it, is not just a game where we are trying to demonstrate our humility by letting Jesus do it all. It is not a game where we "pros" can talk about not being professional because we are already "pros." What we bear witness to is that any person who knows his authority and will operate in the gifts of the Spirit can sit down with one in need—joined with another brother or sister—and participate in the victory for Jesus. You do not have to know techniques or new methods of counseling. You do not have to be clever about putting people at ease. In short, you do not need to be a "pro" to be used by Jesus in setting His people free.

I have seen people who have never counseled before sit in when we had an emergency situation and they have been used by God in the gifts in a way that is amazing. Our secretary, Susie Potter, stepped in one day, never having counseled before or never really wanting to counsel. While we were ministering to a young lady who needed to be set free, Susie was given her first "vision," which confirmed just what was being said as we prayed for the girl. We work with a staff of twenty-five people or so, and many of these workers have specific fields of work other than counseling. Yet, we find that any of them can be called in to share in situations where "two or three gathered in His name" are needed to release the power of the Holy Spirit to heal!

We honestly mean what we say about God teaching us that He does not want professionals any more. He means it when He tells us to ask Him if we have any need to know anything at all—yes, even the name of some demon! God said to us one day, *"I deliver you from the deliverance ministry,"* and we rejoiced, thinking we were through with that dirty business. But He quickly added, *"Oh, no, I mean you will take care of demons in your counseling times. You will see a demon come along, and you will just cast it out and then go right on with the regular counseling and see my people set free! You do not think I'm making you a 'Minister of Deliverance,' do you? You will end up with everybody's garbage, and you will glorify Satan's power, and he will make you work day and night for him!"* We simply don't do that any more! We just take authority over Satan and demand that he go! We don't even argue with him or his demons!

God has shown to us that there is a basic principle that needs to be revealed to His people in His Church! The Body is being purified, and the gifts of the Spirit are beginning to function again in many parts of the Body of Jesus! You who are pentecostals have been affirming this all along, but today we from the mainline denominations are discovering the same truth. Now, as the gifts of the Spirit are beginning to function through us too, we see the potential for ministry just exploding! We are tired of having everybody think that only those who are especially trained in counseling can counsel. The myth of the clergy, of which I have been a part for thirty-five years, is being blown apart! Praise God for this! We are not putting the clergy down. We have proper positions as clergymen, as "shepherds" of the flock, and clergymen are also to remain a vital part of all the ministries. But we believe our principle is best demonstrated in counseling situations. If you want to believe that the gifts of the Spirit are functioning in everyday life, like we claim, just start counseling. It is exciting, for it is clearly *Jesus who does the counseling!* He then connects us into God using the "nine-pronged plug" of the gifts of the Spirit! As we get "plugged into" God, then all His wisdom and knowledge, His faith, His prophetic words, His discernment of spirits, His miracles, His healings, His tongues, and His interpretations get connected to us. So, they become functioning connections to God in every situation where we find ourselves!

We pray for five of the gifts of the Spirit every time we sit down to counsel with an individual. And then people say to us, "Have you found your one gift?" We say, "We have all nine of the gifts when God wants us to use them!" And so do you! Every Christian does who will allow it to happen, who will allow themselves to be connected to the God of the whole universe. The God of the universe loves His people so intimately that He gave His beloved Son, not to judge the world but that the world might be saved through Him! Do you hear that? That is God's mission in this world! It is the mission He calls all believers to be involved in! And for that mission, the great God of all calls to *let the power of the Holy Spirit move!*

That is to us the staggering "mission of the Church" today. You, each one of you—in any church—have the potential of seeing millions come alive in Jesus, *if you will let the power of the Holy Spirit move through you to touch the lives of people all around you!* If you believe Jesus has this power, then let Him use that power in your lives to complete His mission in His world! Don't keep taking the counsel of your fears. Don't keep saying, "I don't know how to talk to people, and they won't believe me anyway! After all, I'm just a layman!" That's all talk that Satan has been putting into the mouths of people to make them think they are humble! That is not being humble, that's being stupid!

Pay careful attention to what Jesus says through Paul, "You are our letter, written in our hearts, known and read by all men; being manifested that you are a letter of Christ, cared for by us, written not with ink, but with the Spirit of the living God, not on tablets of stone, but on tablets of human hearts. And such confidence we have through Christ toward God" (2 Cor. 3:2-4). People say to us, "You make it too big for people! You have to get them used to the long hard haul after they get baptized in the Spirit."

We've gone through the fire. We know what we are talking about. We have been baptized with fire, as well as with the Spirit. How we came out of the fire was not as "great people" but people who know we are nothing, except in Jesus Christ! When He moves through us, all is possible! We really believe that, not just for ourselves but for all believers! We can agree with Paul and say, "Such confidence we have through Christ toward God. Not that we are adequate in ourselves to consider anything as coming from ourselves" (2 Cor. 3:4-5). Hear that, loved ones? *"Our adequacy is from God"!* God lets us have it all!

Have you ever preached in a church where only two people were in the congregation? I did that one time. I was asked to supply for a brother pastor up in Jump River, Wisconsin. I went up there, and only two people showed up. I had driven about 100 miles and even had a flat tire on the way home. I went through the whole service. I even had one man take up the offering, and I was the only one who put anything in!

The same thing happened to one farmer who sat through the whole service as the preacher did what I did. After the service he said, "Preacher, that was very fine. I appreciate you coming. But when I haul hay to my cows out in the pasture and only one cow shows up, I don't dump the whole load on her!"

I have news for you! *God dumps the whole load on you!* That's the truth! If you want to be a follower of Jesus Christ, and you want to have everything He has to offer, you are going to get the whole load dumped on you! You may come crawling out from under that load and say, "Wow, what was that?" That is what He did with us as we moved into the wonderful walk in the Spirit.

In Hebrews 3 and 4 we read how the Israelites did not enter into the rest of God because of their disobedience. They just didn't trust God. They could not combine trust in God with their faith. So they all left their bones in the desert. They did not enter into God's rest at all. They never even got into the Promised Land. As I was teaching on this one time, God told me to write in the margin of my Bible, between chapters three and four, these words: *"If you want Me to stop talking to you, doubt Me."* If you have any doubts in your mind, don't be surprised if God doesn't speak to you! God isn't silent. Stop doubting! Try believing—you'll like it! It's wonderful! It's really exciting to let God's beliefs fill you! The gift of faith is faith to believe like Jesus does. We often pray for the mind of Christ, and we have already discussed this. But just think what this means. If you have Jesus' mind and His Holy Spirit dwelling in you and you are given the gift of faith to believe like Jesus believes, *what is left that you may want?* He has just given us the universe! That's all Jesus offers us! Just everything! People joke about Jesus' demands on them, saying, "What does Jesus want from us? Just everything!" Yes, in exchange for *everything!* The Bible states it clearly, "All that Christ claims as his will belong to all of us as well!" (Rom. 8:17, Phillips). *The New American Standard Bible* says, "We are heirs of God and fellow heirs with Christ." All of this "everything" comes the day we start believing, not the day we finally make it to those "pearly gates."

I call you to the exciting life of walking in the expectancy that every day Jesus is going to do something new! He will show you more power, more energy, more excitement! Read it from God's Word: "If the ministry of death, in letters engraved on stones, came with glory [and it did come with glory, those Ten Commandments!], so that the sons of Israel could not look intently at the face of Moses because of the glory of his face, fading as it was, how shall the ministry of the Spirit fail to be even more with glory?" (2 Cor. 3:7-8). In other words, if the legalism you have given over to through the years and often still hang on to had any glory in it, how shall the ministry of the Spirit fail to be even more glorious? This is our message! The ministry of the Holy Spirit is full of glory! "If the ministry of condemnation [that's the work of the law] has glory, much more does the ministry of righteousness abound in glory"(2 Cor. 3:9). That's what it's all about!

Youare being called to a ministry of the Holy Spirit! When we talk to you and say, "Would you like to counsel in the Spirit," we're saying, "Minister in the Spirit!" And there is glory in it—like you've never seen before. If you think the law and living under it's bondage was good—the "dos and the don'ts," "the look-out-you-are-in-trouble" words, the "fears," and all the other "restrictive admonitions"—I've got good news for you! The glory of moving in the gifts of the Spirit and in the power and the ministry of the Spirit surpasses that glory *so far* that you are going to wonder what you thought was glory at all! Don't stay with the bondage of the law any more. Don't be satisfied with that kind of limited life. God is calling His people to a new concept of life. An old, old idea with a brand-new cover: "For My People In All Churches Everywhere!"

I call you to the new life in the Spirit! Let it happen to you, too! I praise God who had it in His mind to let men like me (who should have been dead years ago as the result of two heart attacks) live to this day to see the glory of God falling upon all people. And I'm believing He will let me live long enough to be raptured with you all!

"Having therefore such a hope, we use great boldness in our speech" (2 Cor. 3:12). People say, "You're awfully bold!" I say to you, "You haven't heard or seen anything yet." God has only started to reveal the wonder of His ministry in the "Last Days" when He is going to bring it all to a perfect conclusion! Those of us who are awake to this work of Jesus, when we see His coming in glory, will know Him. We will be singing His glory, just like we do now. He won't be any stranger to us! For we will know Him as He really is! Hallelujah!

Now the Lord is the Spirit; and where the Spirit of the Lord is, there is liberty. But we all, with unveiled face beholding as in a mirror the glory of the Lord, are being transformed into the same image from glory to glory, just as from the Lord, the Spirit. (2 Cor. 3:17-18)